SUSSEX COUNTY

A History

by

WARREN D. CUMMINGS

with illustrations by

Bill and Bonnie Rutherford

for

The Rotary Club of

Newton, New Jersey

Table of Contents

FOREWORD

The Rotary Club of Newton is proud to be a part of making this history of Sussex County available to you.

Much has transpired during the last 300 years that should be on record about the area in which we live.

We wish to congratulate the author, Warren Cummings, and illustrators, Bill and Bonnie Rutherford, for making the book authentic and interesting.

As strange as it may seem the author says there is very little complete information about Sussex County since 1900. In bringing this history up-to-date it makes a record of the happenings in our lives. As the years go by it will leave a record for another generation.

We are pleased to be able to commemorate New Jersey's 300th birthday by having this book published.

ROTARY CLUB OF NEWTON

August 1, 1964

Chapter I
A County is Born

1. First Arrivals

A pioneer seldom realizes that he is a pioneer. If he is aware that he is the first to visit a new part of the country, it doesn't strike him as particularly important. He just goes about the doing of his job, and it never occurs to him that he's making history.

That was the way it was with the first Europeans to visit Sussex County. Not knowing they were pioneers, they left no records to tell us who they were, when they first came, or what they were looking for. So we must piece together what little evidence we have and make some calculated guesses about our earliest visitors.

Probably they were Dutch, and probably they came from the northeast, pushing up the Walkill from where it enters the Hudson near Kingston. Somewhere near Port Jervis, perhaps, they found the Delaware and inched their way downstream. When did they first come? We cannot say for sure. Perhaps as early as 1654. Almost certainly before 1700.

If they were looking for farmlands they were disappointed. The valley of the Delaware was rough country, heavily wooded, and looked little like the flat and fertile Netherlands for which they were seeking a New World counterpart.

Or perhaps they were looking for metals, and if they were, they were successful. Down the east bank of the Delaware, in what is now Pahaquarry Township of Warren County, they found copper of a grade good enough to make worthwhile the mining and the long haul back to Kingston in New York.

And so began what was to be called the Old Mine Road. The amount of copper it carried was probably not of great importance, but other people besides miners could travel it, and soon the settlers began to move in. They had good Dutch names — Dupuis, Van Campen, Courtright (**Kortrecht**, they spelled it), and Van Auken — and they built homes and cleared farmland.

It is incredible, but they never seemed to worry about where the river went. Every day the Delaware flowed past their homes, and many a floating log disappeared southward without, apparently, exciting their curiosity about where it might be going. Or perhaps they were just too busy to go find out where it went. But when — and this story is very old but unauthenticated — Nicholas Scull pushed up the river from Philadelphia in 1730 to investigate a rumored settlement in the "Meenesink," Samuel Dupuis had no idea where the mouth of the river was. Yet he had lived there long enough to have planted an apple orchard "of size far beyond any near Philadelphia."

1

Apple orchards take a long time to establish and seem to point to a very early settlement of the region. On the other hand, there is an account of a Captain Arent Schuyler, who was sent by the province of New York in 1694 to learn whether the French had been seen in the Minisink country. He came with Indian guides to what he transcribed from the Indian tongue as "Maggahkamieck" and is supposed to be Port Jervis. From there he went to the Minisink, and was told by two Indian sachems and two other Indians that no French or French Indians had been seen. It seems reasonable to suppose that Schuyler would not have depended solely on Indian testimony if there had been Dutch settlements where he could have gone. But it is all conjecture.

When we use the word "Minisink" here, we mean, as the settlers did, the land on both sides of the Delaware as far down as Shawnee, Penna., or the Pahaquarry mines.

Schuyler liked what he saw on this visit, for on May 20, 1697, he obtained a patent for one thousand acres from the Province of New York. The grant seems to have embraced the land between Port Jervis and the Minisink islands, and to have included the islands. It is ironic that with this patent what is now Sussex County first enters documented history as part of New York! That New York thought it had a valid claim was substantiated in 1701 when the inhabitants of Greater and Lower Minisink were given authority to vote in Ulster County by the New York legislature. In 1709 they were considered a part of Orange County, and this claim was not to be relinquished for seventy years.

From this point on the records grow more plentiful. A 1723 deed in the Clerk's office conveys from John Kirkbride of Pennsylvania to John Hutchinson of Philadelphia "1250 acres surveyed by virtue of a warrant dated March 10, 1715." The land was along the Delaware and said to be three miles above the Indian village of Pahaqualin, which Snell's **History of Sussex and Warren Counties** places on a hill below Millbrook.

More records follow. Beginning in 1716, the Reverend Petrus Vas of Kingston made regular trips to the Minisink for baptisms. Later the pastor was the Rev. George Mancius, and by 1737 the settlement along the Delaware had grown enough to support four tiny churches, at what are now Shawnee in Pennsylvania, Walpack, Montague, and Port Jervis. In 1741, a pastor, Johannes C. Fryenmoet, just out of his teens, was named for the settlements, and the community was established.

With the organization of the Minisink churches, the period of predominantly Dutch colonization came to an end. Not that more Dutch were not to come, as Peter Decker came to Deckertown (now Sussex) sometime before 1740. Indeed, the Dutch have not stopped coming, and another large group has arrived since 1945, making possession of a Dutch name a sign that its owner may belong either to one of our oldest or one of our newest Sussex County families!

The next wave of immigration was German. It came up the Delaware, and it was led by Caspar Shafer. Although he was never to lose his strong German accent, he was all American, loved Sussex County, made a personal success here, and played a large part in this County's early development. He was our leading citizen at the time of our beginning, and his story is worth telling here.

2. Our First Citizen

Caspar Shafer came from Germany to Philadelphia. Here he bought, sight unseen, a tract of land along the Paulin's Kill at a spot where Still-water is now. In 1742 he and his father-in-law set out from Philadelphia to find their purchase. They made the whole trip by following first the Delaware and then the Kill until they arrived. The father-in-law soon died, but Caspar dug in with a will. Soon tiring of transporting his grain out by packhorse to the nearest mill, many miles away, he constructed his own mill. Although his first homemade makeshift could grind only three to five bushels of wheat or rye a day, it was ample for the simple needs of the Wintermutes, Snovers, Staleys, Snooks, Couses, and other families, mostly of German origin, who followed him into the section within a few years.

Later he built a larger mill which produced a flour surplus which Shafer loaded onto flatboats and floated down the Paulinskill to the Delaware, and down the Delaware to the Philadelphia market. It was a short-lived experiment, however, for the Paulinskill was much more valuable as a mill stream than it was for Shafer's primitive navigation. The country was filling up, and other milldams soon appeared.

One of the mills was built, though not until after the Revolution, by Caspar's son Peter, at what is now called Paulina, and even later Mark Thompson built a mill still further upstream at a spot which came to be known as Marksboro.

Incidentally, these dams ruined the Paulinskill for shad fishing. When Shafer first came, there had been lots of shad every April.

Caspar (sometimes he spelled it Casper) also had his troubles with the Indians. One night while he was alone a party of savages surrounded his house, yelling and making noisy threats. Annoyed by the racket, Mr. Shafer came out and started across the fields for help. An Indian pursued him — evidently one who didn't know the miller's reputation as the strong-est man for miles around. Shafer lost his temper, grabbed and threw the Indian, then took off his own garters and tied up the warrior. Continuing on to his neighbor's house with drooping stockings, he summoned the help which drove the marauders away.

There is one more Caspar Shafer story which should be told. When the Revolution came, Sussex County, under the new constitution, was allowed three members of the Assembly and one member of the Legislative Council. John Cleves Symmes was the first Councillor, and the Assemblymen were Abia Brown, Thomas Peterson, and Caspar Shafer. Thus he was one of the first representatives of Sussex in the government of our new State. Here is an anecdote of his political career from the address of Benjamin Edsall at the celebration of the one hundredth anniversary of the County's founding in 1853:

"He was a man of few words, but clear-headed and energetic, and wielded much influence in the House. When matters appeared to him to be going wrong, his usual mode of expressing dissent, as I am informed, was to rise in his seat, and with considerable vehemence, and in a strongly-marked German accent, exclaimed, "Tas is nicht recht ! Tas is nicht recht !" and then he would briefly give his views and explanations; whereby the attention of members would be arrested, and not infrequently the current of the proceedings changed."

3. Early Forges and Furnaces

If Sussex County didn't look attractive to the early searchers for farm land, it looked just fine to the prospectors hunting for ore. The first find, as we have seen, was copper, but it was the iron ore that brought more people here in our earliest days. More came to find iron than came for any other reason. Indeed, the iron industry was fundamental to our economy for a hundred years. It may be surprising to know that New Jersey was a leading iron-producing state from 1780 until as late as 1840, and our County's share was large. Most of our first communities grew up around furnaces or forges. Andover, Stanhope, Franklin, Hamburg — these were just a few.

The furnaces made cast iron. This was poured directly from the molten ore into the molds, called "pigs." Cast iron was very hard, but it was full of carbon and consequently brittle and unworkable.

The forges made wrought iron. This was carbon free, or nearly so. Chief feature of a forge was a giant hammer which pounded the heated cast iron to rid it of impurities and to convert it into bars of wrought iron, softer than the cast iron, but tougher and more malleable. Cast iron products were, in those days, chiefly stoves, cannon balls, and the like, while wrought iron was made into anchors, chains, nails, and horseshoes.

Not much steel was made in the early days. To make it took high quality ore, and the tempering process — sudden plunging into cold water when hot — was tricky and delicate. Except for cutlery it was little used.

England was glad to see enterprising Jersey colonists mining iron ore and producing cast iron pigs. There was ore in Britain, but smelting took charcoal, and England's woodlands were nearing exhaustion. Getting iron from America relieved the necessity of buying it from Sweden and Spain.

4

But England wanted no competition from the colonies as far as advanced processes were concerned. All mills for the working of wrought iron were strictly prohibited. Sussex County iron men remembered this prohibition when war came, and it did not increase their sympathy for King George.

In those early days, a bed of iron ore was only one of the items necessary to open a mine. The ore had to be of good quality, for crude methods wouldn't allow low-grade stuff to be handled economically. Here Sussex County was lucky. Our deposits were "hard" ores (blue magnetite and red hematite, to be technical about it), and in their day they were far and away the best quality around.

At Andover the two kinds were mixed to produce an exceptionally tough iron which made good steel. From the Andover shaft (really a great pocket rather than a true shaft) was to come the iron for the first railroad rails that wouldn't split. In 1770 men thought the Andover iron would last forever. Ninety years later it was worked out.

Franklin's iron was the easiest to mine anywhere around. One man could get out two or three tons a day, not bad when one remembers that the miner had only old-fashioned gunpowder to blast with.

What held down production in the earliest days was hauling — what to do with the ore after it was brought out. This difficulty was so great that it was usually necessary to have the forge and furnace close to the mine.

But much more than ore was needed. There had to be a lively stream for water power and, most important of all, there had to be lots of wood.

The water power ran the bellows for the strong air blast the furnace needed. The ore was mixed with limestone for a "flux" and heated with charcoal. As it turned into a molten mass, the impurities rose to the top and were drawn off, while the liquid metal flowed from a tap in the bottom.

But it was wood to make charcoal that was the early iron man's biggest problem. His furnace ate charcoal in great gulps. It required twelve thousand acres of woodland to keep a furnace going for twenty years until cutting could start again.

January to April was off-season at the furnaces. The iron managers had to let the furnaces cool off to renew the firebrick. Anyway, the stream which ran the blower was likely to be frozen over. But when running at capacity, a good furnace could turn out twenty-five tons a week, seven hundred in a year.

The forges needed an even better water supply, for the hammers weighed five hundred pounds and were geared to a water wheel. It took a steady flow to keep the hammer pounding the reheated pig iron which had been brought from the forge to the block by tongs. Sometimes the wrought iron which resulted was called bar iron, for that was the form it took. As the hammer fell, the boom could be heard for miles.

Around these forges or furnaces grew up little self-contained communities. There were such villages at Stanhope, Lockwood, Waterloo, Andover, Ogdensburg, Franklin, Canisteer, Russia, and other spots. The same dam which ran the blower or trip-hammer frequently powered a grist or saw mill as well.

Central in the typical iron community was the home of the manager. This was usually the most imposing dwelling in town. There was sometimes a company store and almost always a barracks-like dormitory for the workers.

These workers were of two sorts. There were, naturally, some slaves, but these were never very numerous in Sussex County. And there were ordinary paid laborers, but the big source of supply was indentured servants, and of these the local iron centers had a great many. They were repaying for their passage to this country by agreeing to work for seven years for food, shelter, and very little else. Most of the indentured servants came from England or from Germany. The Germans were highly respected for their industry; in fact, early advertisers sometimes specified "those who are German or can work in the German way."

The early iron works at Waterloo must have employed a very large number of indentured servants, or the treatment there must have been particularly bad, for scarcely an issue of the New York or Philadelphia newspapers in the 1760's and '70's but contains a description of a runaway servant from this place. Apprehenders were admonished to "take him up and deliver him to the nearest jail," and the advertiser would guarantee all expenses for board and lodging, and a liberal reward besides.

Typical of the early mining operations in Sussex County, although bigger than most, was that of Allen and Turner, a couple of enterprising business men from Philadelphia whose pre-Revolutionary ventures are fabulous in their diversity and range. They entered the Sussex County scene in 1760 with the purchase of eleven thousand acres of promising mineral deposits and heavy timber. They named their purchase Andover for Turner's old home town in England. Allen had already been honored by the naming of Allentown in Pennsylvania, another project of the partners. The first manager of the Sussex County operation was Colonel John Hackett, and before long he was to have a town named for him!

Because there was some doubt of Allen and Turner's enthusiasm for the cause of the colonies, and because of the immense value of the workings, the new U. S. government took over in 1778 and ran the development until the end of the war. It is highly probable that one of the factors contributing to Washington's bivouacs at Morristown was a desire to protect this strategically important prize.

It is commonly asserted that the Andover works turned out cannon balls and other shot for the Continental Army, but there is no direct evidence of this. It is, as a matter of fact, highly doubtful, for the Andover iron was of such superior quality that such a use would be a waste. Most of the Andover iron probably ended up as steel.

The heyday of the forges and furnaces was over by 1800. Coal was coming out of the Lehigh Valley, and the cheapness and greater effectiveness of coal smelting gradually put the charcoal burners into eclipse. Andover was to have another brief moment of iron production a generation later, but that story must wait for a later chapter.

4. June 8, 1753

The iron men and the farmers and the indentured servants had been flocking into northwestern New Jersey since 1740. Most of the movement was north from Philadelphia, for not only was that city the metropolis of those days, it was the center of Quakerism, and all this section was claimed and parcelled out by the Penns. As the population grew, the subdivisions began: did you realize that the earliest settlers of this part of the state were under the jurisdiction of the "High Sheriff of ye Countye of Burlington"? Then the northern section of Burlington was broken off and called Hunterdon; a little later Morris was made from northern Hunterdon and our forefathers belonged to **that**.

A few more years passed, and our ancestors began objecting to the long and difficult trip to Morristown every time they had county business to transact. There were enough of them by 1753 to make their objections heard all the way to the capital, and Sussex was set off from Morris. In 1824, Sussex was divided for the last time, and Warren County was set off from it.

And so, on June 8, 1753, was passed "An Act for erecting the upper Parts of Morris County in New-Jersey into a separate County, to be called the County of Sussex, and for building a Courthouse and Gaol in each of the said Counties."

In our County neither the court house nor the jail was built for some time, and early court sessions and meetings of the chosen freeholders were held in private homes and taverns. The first meeting of what corresponds to our Board of Freeholders was held in Johnsonsburg (remember, Warren was part of Sussex then) on the first day of spring in 1754. The meeting place was the home of Samuel Green. Those present at that first meeting: Abram VanCampen, Jonathan Pettit, Thomas Woolverton, Richard Lundy, Jr., Robert Wilson, Samuel Wilson, Joseph Hull, Joseph Willits, Derik Westbrook, Cornelius Westbrook.

At the next meeting, a year later, decision was reached to build a jail on Green's land, and a log "gaol" was speedily constructed. Of the county's first public edifice it has been said that it was famous for "the universal complaint of the sheriffs that they were unable to keep prisoners in, and the universal complaint of the prisoners that they would not stay in unless the sheriff would keep the sheep out."

It seems hard to believe today, but these first county officials had been in office for over a year before they got around to doing anything about taxes. Then they selected Thomas Woolverton of Huntsville for county collector, and set one hundred pounds to be collected. About a third of this was to pay for the jail; the rest was to pay bounties on wolves and panthers. No roads; no bridges. A county budget was just that simple two hundred years ago!

The county was at first divided into four townships: Walpack and Newton included all of present Sussex except for what is now Stillwater and Green; Hardwick and Greenwich took in all of what is now Warren County, plus Stillwater and Green. A year later, 1754, Wantage was formed. In 1759 Montague was established by royal patent. In 1762 Sandyston was set off from Walpack. The other townships came considerably later.

The important fact is that it was the Newton township, comprising most of the eastern part of the County, which was the most populous, carried the largest share of the tax burden, and was the most influential. When the question of a permanent court house came up, this influence made itself felt.

It was in 1761 that the legislature again authorized the building of a court house and specified a definite spot in Newton Township. It is probable that the choice of a site was influenced by Jonathan Hampton, who owned about twenty-five hundred acres of what is now the town of Newton, and who gave the land on which the Court House was eventually built. He also gave land for a church. Could he have foreseen that a town would grow up here and make the rest of his plot very valuable? I suspect that he could.

Here the Court House was built and stood until 1847, when fire destroyed it. After some strong pressure to move to a new location, the present Court House was constructed on the same site.

5. Indian Troubles

With the crushing defeat of General Braddock in July, 1775, the settlements to the east lay unprotected. The French knew it. Sensing the value

8

of attack, they sent the Indians raiding far in advance of the line they had chosen to hold. Bright with war paint and eager for loot, the braves struck swiftly, repeatedly, and with greater and greater boldness. From beyond the Ohio and down from Canada they flicked bloody thrusts to the Susquehanna, to the Lehigh, to the Delaware.

On November 26, 1755, a letter from Abram VanCampen of Walpack, published in the New York **Mercury**, described the burning of a Moravian town in Pennsylvania, the murder of the inhabitants, and the burning in the night of a house only six miles from the river. The goose quill of the writer dripped panic with the ink. He cried for aid against a foe which had surrounded the County and for which the feeble defenses of the residents would prove no deterrent whatever.

New Jersey and Sussex County moved quickly upon receipt of the news. Within an hour of hearing it, Governor Belcher had ordered Colonel John Anderson into Pennsylvania with one hundred Sussex militia, and next day there were reinforcements from all over the northern half of the state. By Christmas the legislators, in special session, had raised ten thousand pounds for frontier defense and provided for the erection of four block houses (the number was later increased) within the borders of the County and along the river. The first, Fort Reading, was twelve miles above Easton; the second at Colonel VanCampen's, sixteen miles further up the river; the third, Fort Walpack, six miles further; six miles above Walpack the fourth; then one at Fort Nomanock, eight miles distant, and others above. But even this commendable dispatch was too late. Events happened quickly.

In May, 1756, a small war party burned the house of Captain Hunt at Hunt's Pond in Greenwich Township and carried off Hunt's younger brother and a Negro servant.

A day later, the same party burned Anthony Swartout's home near Swartswood Lake, scalped him, killed four of his children, and took two more with them.

A year later thirteen Indians rushed into the house of Nicholas Cole in Montague one afternoon while he was away, seized his wife, tomahawked his son-in-law, and scalped three of his children. One of these, a four-year-old girl, was impaled with spears before her mother's eyes. Mrs. Cole and one of her sons were taken prisoner. On the same day a man was scalped in a field near Minisink Island, and two German settlers were taken prisoner near Montague. But Cole, returning home to a scene of horror and desolation, aroused the garrison at Fort Nomanock and waylaid the Indians as they crossed the river at two in the morning. At a shot the Indians fled, leaving Mrs. Cole and her son unharmed. Of the two German settlers, no further word.

A month later this same section had another alarm when a Sergeant VanTile and nine soldiers had a sharp skirmish with about twenty-five

booty-laden Indians preparing to cross the river into Pennsylvania. An Indian was killed; the rest dropped their loot and retreated. Both VanTile and a seventeen-year-old named Titsort, who killed a famous Indian raider named John Armstrong, were rewarded by the legislature with twenty Spanish dollars and a silver medal.

It must be admitted that all the crimes were not committed by Indians. The settlers fought back, often with murder and cruelty. Immediately Tom Quick comes to mind. What was fact and what is fancy in the Tom Quick

legend cannot be separated now. Quick certainly killed some Indians, but he was a lawless boaster, and the kindest criticism of his tales is that they were unreliable.

There are, however, some grim items in the record which suggest the frustration, exasperation, and ugly mood of our ancestors. When Swartout was murdered at Swartswood Lake, the governor offered rewards for the capture or killing of male Indians over fifteen years of age and for the capture of children under fifteen regardless of sex. You brought in an Indian's scalp to prove the killing, and the state paid you one hundred and thirty dollars.

In 1758 a new governor came out from England teeming with ideas. He was going to line the Delaware with blockhouses and patrol between them with hounds several times a day. In this way, if any Indians crossed the river, he would know it soon. "Probably," he said, "before their scent, which is very strong by their using bear's grease, is gone off the ground."

But the new governor was shrewd enough to know that the only way to real peace was to make a deal. This he did in Easton in 1758, in a Great Council with all the interested tribes. All Indian claims north of the Raritan were settled for one thousand dollars.

The Indians kept their word. Peace returned to the Sussex hills. The frontier guard was disbanded. The governor happily established the township of Montague, "a country," said he, "that a year ago no one would venture to live in."

6. Revolutionary Days

Fourteen months before the Declaration of Independence was signed in Philadelphia, Sussex County already had cut itself free from the control of the Crown. Here, dated May 10, 1775, is the Board of Freeholders' own declaration of Independence:

"**Ordered,** That the Sheriff shall be paid the sum of four pounds, it being money advanced by him to discharge the Judges' expenses of two Supreme Courts; and this Board orders that, from henceforth no Judges' expenses shall be paid by this County."

Our ancestors were like that. They didn't burn any tea. They didn't make a lot of noise. They just stopped paying.

They had talked enough earlier. In 1774 they had met at the Court House, citizens as well as Freeholders, and after much discussion approved a resolution drawn by John Cleves Symmes of Walpack. Among other items, the resolution announced their decision to

a. be taxed only with their consent
b. boycott British goods

c. join with the other counties in choosing representatives to a Continental Congress

d. abide by the decisions of this Congress

e. appoint a committee of correspondence to keep them in touch with what was happening elsewhere.

By the summer of 1775, two governments were functioning side by side in New Jersey. At the head of the legal government was the king-appointed governor. At the head of the extralegal government was the Provincial Congress, to which went delegates from a County Committee of Safety, which was composed, in turn, of representatives from township committees of safety.

Sussex County's committee was busy giving everyone an opportunity to swear allegiance to the Continental Congress and support to the revolutionary committee. Those who tried to remain loyal to the king were "persuaded" in various ways. One method of persuasion was suggested by Symmes's motion, carried by the Committee in August, 1775, which proposed that any Tories "who shall asperse any of the friends of liberty, or speak contemptuously or disrespectfully of the Continental or Provincial Congresses," should be visited by a captain of militia in company with five or six men, and if "they refuse to retract or express sorrow and contrition" they were to be brought before the County Committee "to be dealt with according to his or their deserts."

It is going to be necessary to make considerable use of the name of John Cleves Symmes if we are to give any account of Sussex County in the Revolution. He suddenly emerges to stand along side of Caspar Shafer — both of them were members of the Committee of Safety — as a leading citizen. Let's tell something here of this outstanding patriot.

John Cleves Symmes was born on Long Island in 1742 and moved to Walpack in 1760. He owned several hundred acres, including the site of the present village of Walpack Center. Educated for the law, he apparently never practiced, but threw himself with zeal into the American cause and organized his own battalion. In the fall of 1776 he took it to Morristown, where he and his men joined a brigade under Colonel Jacob Ford.

Symmes distinguished himself in an action at Springfield in December, 1776, but mere command of a battalion could not keep busy a man with his boundless energy and tireless intellect. Interspersed with his military service was a term as judge of the County court and as a member of the committee which drafted New Jersey's first state constitution.

In 1777, he resigned from his army post to become Associate Justice of New Jersey's first Supreme Court. Somewhere, too, in all this activity he found time to court and wed the daughter of William Livingston, our first governor after independence. She was Symmes's third wife. The first two were dead — probably from exhaustion in trying to keep up with him!

In 1787, Symmes formed a syndicate which bought two million acres of choice Ohio land from the government and went into the real estate business. One of his partners in the scheme was the New Jersey soldier, Gen. Jonathan Dayton, whose name was made secure in the naming of Dayton, Ohio.

In this venture Symmes was not so lucky. He too picked a site for a city, named it Symmes, laid out streets and lots, and waited for customers who never came. The trouble was that fifteen miles away another new town was getting all the business. Its name was Cincinnati. So Symmes moved to Cincinnati, served as judge of the Northwest Territory, saw his daughter married to an up-and-coming young soldier named William Henry Harrison.

Symmes was never to know that one day his son-in-law would be President of the United States. In 1814 he died at Harrison's Ohio home, aged 72. It took a cancer to kill him.

No battle of the Revolution was fought on Sussex County soil. But if the war didn't come to us — I'm overlooking an Indian raid in Montague in 1777 — Sussex men certainly went to the wars. Our soldiers were of three types:

First, the regular army men, many of whom were with General William Maxwell and his brother Captain John at Trenton, Princeton, Brandywine, and other battlefields.

Second, the militia, the Minute Men who repelled Indian attacks at our borders and in nearby New York and Pennsylvania. It was men from the Second Sussex Militia, mostly from Hardyston and Wantage, who fought Brant, the Indian raider, at the Battle of Minisink in Orange County, N. Y., and lost at least six on a July day in 1778.

And third, and not to be ignored, those who remained loyal to the King, and either fought in Loyalist regiments with the British or as guerillas harassed Washington's supply lines and terrorized towns and villages far from the active front of fighting.

During Washington's two winters at Morristown these supplies from Sussex County were extremely important, and another humble contribution we made to Washington's army was inaugurated by Thomas Anderson, of Newton, of whom we will have more to say later. Anderson distributed broken-down cavalry horses to local farms to be nursed back to health. So successful were he and the cooperating farmers in this service that Sussex County became a leading convalescent center for the horseflesh of the Continental Army.

And what about Moody? The Tory raider was our County's most romantic figure in the Revolution. But a large part of the romance is founded on legend, much of it of Moody's own making, for he wrote a book

14

in England after the war in which there may be a grain of truth, but not much more. The facts seem to be only these.

1. His name was James Moody, not Bonnell Moody, as he is called in some old stories.
2. He entered a Tory regiment as a private, served a year, was made an ensign. In 1781 he was raised to lieutenant and later was sent to England.
3. He was once a prisoner at West Point.
4. The whole period of his activity in the County was about one year, early 1780 to early 1781. His purpose here was to recruit for His Majesty's N. J. Volunteers.

All else is either fiction or is completely unverifiable. But a shrewd guess would be that there must have been some Tory sympathizers around, or Moody would not have stayed so long or gone so long uncaught. The stories about the jail-break, Moody's Rock, and the other escapades, **ought** to be true. Unfortunately, such evidence as there is suggests that the stories were created long after the Revolution was over.

Chapter II
A County Grows Up

1. Early Schools

The schools were late in coming. Not only was population sparse, but the mining communities had a smaller percentage of children than other towns of comparable size. And life was hard for the children there were: by the time a boy was big enough to go to school he was big enough to help some.

The ministers did some teaching. Some of them were college trained; they gathered about them the most promising youngsters of their congregations and gave the boys (why should a girl have education?) a start. Often it was a labor of love, but sometimes the pastors could help out their salaries by charging tuition.

When a school building was built in the eighteenth century, it was usually a log cabin, sixteen feet or so square, with a board roof and battened with saw mill slabs nailed oval side out. The chimney was of stick and clay construction. There was one door and one window. If the door had to be closed because of the cold, the light was pretty feeble.

Such schools as these would operate sporadically. An itinerant teacher would come by, open the building, and "keep school" for as long as the townfolk would pay, usually three months at a stretch. These schools gave only the barest rudiments — the teachers were rarely equipped to give more — and if a lad showed aptitude, and his parents could afford it, he would be put into the home of some New York, Paterson, or Elizabeth minister or physician with two or three other boys to prepare for college.

Almost the first real school of permanence in the County was established in 1825 at Newton by the Rev. Clarkson Dunn of Christ Church. Then, in 1828, the Rev. Edward Allen opened the Clove school where he advertised instruction in "Latin, English grammar, and astronomy."

Two years later Allen opened a more pretentious school at Harmonyvale, near Hamburg, with fifty boarders as well as day students. The Deckertown school followed in 1833, the year which also saw the establishment of the "Wantage Select School," which later became Mount Retirement Seminary and was to endure until 1865. Sometime before 1833, Willard Barrows had opened an academy at Branchville.

But the story of early schools in Sussex County is so much the story of William Rankin that we should tell about him without further delay.

Rankin was born in Greeneville, Tennessee, and from somewhere acquired a burning ambition to go to Yale. So one day he started out — he just walked northeast. How many months or years he was on the road we do not know. We do know that he stopped here and there to teach school for a spell whenever his money ran low, and we can guess that he read avidly every book that he came across in his journey.

He appears in these parts first in 1828 at Johnsonsburg, in the new county of Warren. It is said that when he inquired about the possibilities for starting a school, the Johnsonsburg citizenry was convulsed with mirth, for this ragged wayfarer gave every appearance of being the simplest of backwoods hicks. In a spirit of fun, they called in Dr. Roderick Byington to test the capabilities of the applicant. The doctor was about the only resident with any claim to an education.

You guessed it. It was the doctor who bowed in awe before the learning of the new schoolmaster. One term later William Rankin was with Clarkson Dunn at the Christ Church school and with Allen at the Clove. We are not sure which position he held first, but at last his great opportunity came, he was off to Yale. But in a year he was back. Either he was disappointed at what he found or his money ran out, and a long and distinguished career in education was about to begin.

In 1838, after assisting other men, he rented a vacant building in Deckertown and advertised the opening of his school. On opening day he found just one pupil. His name was John A. Whittaker, and he was from Unionville. John was later to be a bank president, which thought might have consoled Rankin had he known it. As it was, he swallowed his disappointment and went to work. In a matter of weeks his fame had spread, his school had grown to twenty, and at the end of ten years he could count one thousand different students who had studied with him for a longer or shorter period.

William Rankin was a master teacher who inspired his students with the desire to teach. We can with some justice claim for him and for Sussex County New Jersey's first normal school, actually if not in name. In the twenty-two years between Rankin's beginning in Deckertown and the opening of the first State Normal School in Trenton, four or five hundred—think of it!—teachers had gone out from Rankin's school to teach in New Jersey and in nearby New York and Pennsylvania.

William Rankin stayed with us until he was an old man. Then he moved to Mendham, where he died, still teaching until the end.

There were others of lesser renown. Ephraim Woodruff, who taught the school at Ogdensburg about 1806 was long remembered for two great passions. For many years his former pupils would argue about which he loved most: telling stories of his adventures in the Revolution or whipping the students. He had great enthusiasm for both.

In 1821 Charles Worrell was teaching in a log hut just north of Swartswood village. This school had not even a chimney; the smoke found its way out through a hole in the roof. At McAfee an early instructor was John Hammill, who rode a fine horse named School Boy. What his pupils remembered with distaste was that he held school every other Saturday. Over near Walpack Center, Jonathan Thompson was keeping a school as early as 1800. He used to wear two or three pairs of spectacles at the same time, his pupils said, and maintained stoutly that his sight improved in direct ratio to the number of pairs he wore.

From Montague we receive an inkling of what schooling cost. Here, at the beginning of the nineteenth century, parents paid twelve shillings (about three dollars) for every child for a period of twelve weeks. But a teacher did not receive all of this in cash. Folks with little ready money or with large families frequently boarded the schoolmaster in lieu of tuition payments.

As you will notice, all of these dates are after 1800. Of earlier schools we know almost nothing. As early as 1731, a gift of ground for a school in the Mine Road settlement had been made, but certainly no building was erected until much later. The Rev. Joseph Shaw, Moravian missionary to the western part of the County, did some teaching in 1746-47. There was a school at the corner of Liberty and High streets in Newton for a time before 1789. Incidentally, Dunn's academy in Newton, the County's first school of any permanence, was located on what is now called Division Street.

2. How People Traveled

Even before the coming of the first colonists, this region had had one highway. This was the Minisink Path, which began on the shore at the mouth of the Shrewsbury River, crossed the Raritan, went through what is now Springfield, and then northwestward by way of Morristown and Lafayette, and on to Minisink Island in the Delaware. But this was an Indian trail unsuited for wagons, and played little part in our County's history.

Except for the Mine Road, which had fallen into disuse except locally, roads up until 1800 received no attention at all. After that they became a township responsibility. Many men worked out all or part of their taxes by labor on the township's roads. Being farmers, both overseers and workers would do nothing until after corn-planting time. Then they pitched in to get the appropriation used up and their debt worked off during the lull. By winter the roads were as bad as ever, and there was no money until the next town meeting in the spring.

Snow plowing was never thought of. A good fall of snow, packed down by horses and sleighs, was a boon to speedy and easy travel. Farmers waited for snow to do their heaviest carting. People saved up visits to distant friends and relatives until after a big fall of snow. If drifts were encountered, the travelers simply took down the rail fences and detoured through the fields. In big snows such as Sussex County had in 1835-36, April 1854, January 1857, December 1872, and the blizzard of March 1888, everybody turned out and shoveled out the worst spots by hand.

It was in 1801 that a great wave of road building began. The turnpike companies started it. These companies operated in this way: they surveyed a route between two likely points, sold stock in their company to potential users along the way, and built a twenty-four foot (usually) road of dirt and gravel. Turnpike gates were installed along the way at points of access, and the tolls collected paid off the investment, maintained the road, and returned the owners a handsome profit. At least in theory (and in the advertising) that was what happened. And some of the toll roads were enormously successful. There were many, however, that never realized their projectors' fond hopes. Many were inadequately capitalized, and the tolls, though small, were unpopular with the farmers. The companies found it necessary to plant posts and dig ditches opposite the toll houses to prevent teams from turning out around the gates. A good saddle horse that could jump the gate made his owner a local hero.

The depression of 1817, plus the diverting of freight traffic to canals, steamboats, and ultimately to railroads finished many of the turnpikes. But they made a furore while they lasted. Between 1801 and 1819 the legislature gave authority for fifty turnpike roads. By coincidence, both number one and number fifty ran through Sussex County. Twenty-eight of the fifty were wholly or partially built, twenty-two were never begun.

The first turnpike road in New Jersey was the Morris Turnpike, authorized March 9, 1801, "from Elizabethtown, through Morristown and Newton, over the Minisink Mountain at Culver's Gap, to the Delaware, opposite Milford." It was completed in 1807, and was a link in the great highway that ran on to Binghamton, Buffalo, and the West via the Great Lakes. So it played a part in the development of Illinois, Ohio, Michigan, and the other new states and territories into which a flood of new pioneers were pouring. Sussex County folks caught the fever too. In the two years 1836-37, for one illustration, thirty-five families which attended the North Church moved west, nearly crippling that congregation for a time.

The turnpike was a tremendous benefit to the County. It was our first opening to eastward, our first chance to freight out our iron and butter by other than pack train. It provided the first opportunity to import more than a token of anything but the rigid necessities, and the resulting luxuries took away much of the County's primitive and pioneer look.

Finally, it broke definitely our last bond with Philadelphia. Many of our earliest settlers had come from there, and the old ties were strong. Now "New Ark," Elizabeth, and New York were to be our markets and our shopping centers.

Quick to take advantage of the new turnpike's possibilities was Isaac Basset, a Newton hotel keeper, who with two partners established the first stage route; it ran from Newton to Elizabeth by way of Morristown. This stage began operation August 15, 1808. Leaving Newton at nine in the morning, a traveler could make New York by noon the next day. The stage ran but once a week. In 1824 stages began running three times a week in each direction between New York and Owego by way of Newton, and in 1825 it was possible to take a stage daily to either Buffalo or New York.

One of the most successful of all the turnpikes ran from Paterson to Hamburg. The company which built it was organized in 1806, and the stages ran from 1810 until the coming of the railroad. The last stage on the Hamburg Turnpike ran June 29, 1872. The Union Turnpike began at Dover and ran through Sparta to Lafayette, where the stage made a stop at the famous Predmore tavern. From there it ran on to Augusta and joined the Morris Turnpike.

From very early, perhaps as early as 1760, a road ran from Newton through Deckertown and on to Goshen, and the Newton-Sussex part (Sussex and Deckertown are the same place, remember) was later developed by a turnpike company. But the turnpikes seldom lived up to their promises to provide a high quality road surface. In 1833 Thomas Gordon wrote with some disgust that he did not recollect seeing five continuous miles of stone surface in his travels into every corner of the state.

Meanwhile, the demand for cheap and easy transport was turning men's attention to the canals. Although the Morris Canal touched but one corner of Sussex County, it did have an influence on the temporary revival of the iron industry in Andover, it provided an outlet for our farm products, and construction brought us our first considerable number of Irish immigrants.

The man who first envisioned this most improbable of all canals was George McCulloch of Morristown, who got the idea while fishing in Lake

Hopatcong. Why not, thought he, use this lake as a link in a canal system to connect the Delaware and the Hudson? Not only would it bring Lehigh Valley coal to New York, but it might do something for the iron industry in Sussex and Morris counties. The forges and furnaces here had dropped in number from nearly a hundred to less than forty, and Morris County was feeling the pinch equally. The decline in business was the result largely of the fact that it was actually cheaper to bring a ton of iron from Russia to New York than to bring it from northwestern New Jersey.

The realization that the point at which he was fishing was more than nine hundred feet above sea level, and that getting a loaded canal boat up a rise of nine hundred feet and then getting it down again was quite a trick never seemed to bother George McCulloch at all. There would be some locks in his canal, but McCulloch's solution for the lifting problem was the inclined plane. As the boat reached the foot of the plane, it floated onto a "cradle," a sort of railroad car, which was on tracks at the bottom of the canal. Then the cradle with its boat aboard was pulled up the slope by a chain on a windlass. Once at the top, it coasted down the other side, where the cradle submerged again and the canal boat floated off to resume its more conventional mode of travel.

There were troubles. The canal cost too much; it was too shallow and narrow to accommodate boats with real payloads; the new Delaware and Raritan Canal got most of the coal carrying business; the speculators in control were more interested in manipulating the company's stock than in developing the company's canal. But from 1844 until 1866 the canal carried some of our farm produce eastward to market while our iron ore went to Phillipsburg and Trenton.

But the railroads were coming, and the canals were doomed. As early as 1836 there had been talk of a railroad in both Deckertown and Newton. However, it was 1847 before talk turned to action, and the new owners of the Andover mine incorporated the Sussex Mine R. R. to connect Andover with the Morris Canal and with the Morris and Essex R. R., pushing west from Dover.

When, in 1852, the citizens of Newton petitioned for an extension of the Sussex Mine R. R. to Newton and for its opening to general traffic, they were asked to put up $100,000 cash and to buy the right of way. They moved fast. In three weeks they had promise to all of the right of way from Newton to Andover except for three owners. Another month, and they had raised $90,000 and started construction. In ten weeks from the start of the campaign for funds the whole amount had been raised. And on the twenty-seventh of November, 1854, the first locomotive arrived at the Newton station. Regular service began December 11, 1854, and brought a wave of prosperity to Newton and vicinity, which people were quick to appreciate. When the big snow of January, 1857, cut off rail service, eighty Newtonians turned out with shovels and cleared the tracks from the station to Drake's pond, where they met the railroad's gang working northward.

The first train to Lafayette from Newton ran January 1, 1869, and by July of that year service was opened through to Branchville.

At the same time, the people in Deckertown had been agitating for their own rail connection. As early as 1832 the New Jersey, Hudson & Delaware R. R. had been chartered, but the proposed road, which was to connect the Hudson with the Delaware, was never begun. Other hopefuls organized companies called the New Jersey Western R. R. Co. and the Sussex Valley R. R. Co., but they too were just names on stock certificates.

Finally, after nearly forty years, all of these concerns reorganized into a new corporation called the New Jersey Midland, and in 1870 work was begun at Deckertown. In 1871 a train ran from Newton to Deckertown over the Sussex and Midland. Then another section joined Franklin and Unionville. The next year the first train ran over the New Jersey Midland all the way to Jersey City.

People here had a firm faith, in the decade before the Civil War and for some time afterward, in the power of the freight car to remake our future. Sussex County was going to be the food-producing center for the whole metropolitan area. Everybody was going to get rich. This was the general tone of the speeches and the editorials. They did not yet realize that those same freight cars could also bring the more cheaply produced foods of the South and the Middle West.

3. Some Great Lawyers

One of the reasons why Sussex County was first established was that our citizens found it inconvenient to make the long trip to Morristown to conduct their legal business and to serve on juries. The earliest court sessions in our County were held in various taverns, and the lawyers who tried the cases were all from other sections. No lawyer hung out his shingle here until the Court House was built in the 1760's, and then came Thomas Anderson.

Anderson was much more than a lawyer. He was clerk of the Committee of Safety, and he was, during the Revolution, Assistant Deputy Quartermaster General, in which job he was to keep flowing to Trenton, Morristown, and New Brunswick a constant stream of flour, chopped feed, and other supplies. He became our first surrogate and stayed in that post until 1807.

Perhaps our most gifted lawyer of those earliest years was Robert Ogden, Jr., whose ancestors founded Elizabeth, and whose father, Speaker of the province's House of Assembly, first settled in Ogdensburg in 1777.

Robert graduated from Princeton at nineteen and began practice in Elizabeth. A disabled right arm kept him out of the army, and in 1786, his asthma growing worse and his aging father needing his support, he came to Ogdensburg permanently. With him came his growing family. His first wife died at the birth of their fifth child, and he had married her sister and fathered six more. One of the sons was to be a justice of the supreme court of Louisiana, a grandson was to be governor. Robert's life was one of semi-retirement, but he practiced law occasionally, served the County in the legislature, and spent his last years at his daughter's home in Hamburg.

A cousin of Robert Ogden, Jr., was Job S. Halsted, who was born in Elizabeth in 1774. Coming to Newton as a young man, he practiced law in Sussex County for more than fifty years. He was a gentleman who maintained courtly manners long after knee breeches and powdered hair had given way to the cruder forms of the days of our national growth. He lived until 1844, a consistent Whig (he voted for the nomination of Henry Clay as a delegate to the convention of 1832) in a County of Jeffersonian Democrats.

The other leading lawyer of our growing-up years was Martin Ryerson, whose grandfather had first seen the county as a surveyor of the East-West Jersey line. Martin was born in Hamburg in 1815 and graduated from Princeton in 1833. His fame today rests securely on his part in the state constitutional convention of 1844, which gave New Jersey a governmental structure which was to endure for more than a hundred years.

Perhaps Martin Ryerson's outstanding contributions to the 1844 constitution were his insistence on the rights of naturalized citizens to full citizenship and his stubborn fight to keep the Court of Errors and Appeals from becoming entirely monopolized by lawyers. He thought that decisions in what was then our state's highest tribunal of appeal should be decided on the basis of justice and common sense rather than upon some legal quibble.

But his greatest fight he lost. Valiantly he battled against the clause which forbade a governor to succeed himself. He argued that to make any man constitutionally ineligible was to deny to the people the right to vote for whomever they pleased. But the no-succession rule was put into the 1844 constitution over Ryerson's protests.

A hundred years later a new constitution was adopted. Ryerson, dead nearly fifty years, won this time. Now our governor can be re-elected.

I have a strong suspicion that perhaps Daniel Haines was the greatest citizen our County has yet produced. Born in New York City in 1801, his mother brought him often to visit his Grandfather Ogden at Ogdensburg,

and he grew to love the country. After his graduation from Princeton in 1820, Daniel took up the practice of law in Hamburg and almost immediately went into politics. Naturally he was a Democrat; one indication of Democratic strength in the County then is shown by the 1824 Presidential vote in Vernon Township: **every vote** was for Jackson!

Haines entered public life as a member of the New Jersey Senate, and made such a reputation for calmness and leadership in a minor hysteria called the Broad Seal War that he first became Governor in 1843. His second term was 1847-50. During his first term New Jersey adopted a new constitution. In his second term he turned his energies toward the training of teachers, and the first State Normal School opened at Trenton in 1855 as a monument to his vision and perseverance.

Some of his interests in the next twenty-five years included two terms on the supreme court bench, the trusteeship of Princeton. He went abroad to attend meetings dedicated to prison reform. And nearest to his heart was his office as elder at the North Church, and later at the Hamburg Presbyterian Church, which he helped to found.

His long life had its sorrows as well as triumphs. After seventeen years his first wife died. One son, Capt. Thomas Haines of the 1st N. J. Cavalry, lost his life chasing Stonewall Jackson up the Shenandoah Valley in 1862. After this, Daniel Haines spent less and less time at the big house in Hamburg (his other son was also away in service) and more in Newark, where much of his law practice now was. It was here that he married when he was sixty-four years old.

He was to live another twelve years and to die when he was seventy-six. His health had been failing; he had turned down an invitation to represent American Presbyterians at a church convention in Scotland when death came suddenly on the evening of January 26, 1877. Of the thousands of words that were written and said about him, his abilities, and his contributions to his state and country, perhaps the shortest is also the most complete. A lawyer who had tried many cases against Haines the attorney and before Haines the judge said, "What a beautiful exemplification of the Christian gentleman he was!"

4. The Fowlers of Franklin

First of the Fowlers was Sam, born at Newburgh, N. Y., in 1779. By 1801 he was finished with his medical studies in Philadelphia and had settled in Hamburg. In 1808 he married, but after the birth of a daughter and the death of his wife, he moved.

His new home was on what was called The Plains, the flat land between Franklin and North Church. Here Dr. Fowler built a dam and erected a grist mill, fulling mill, blacksmith shop, and tannery. Then he built several houses for the workers who manned his enterprises, and named his little settlement Franklin, after his favorite historical figure. It was after this move to Franklin that Dr. Sam Fowler found himself. In 1816, aged thirty-six, he married into the Ogden family (everybody seems to have done that!) and raised six children. His medical practice grew; he went into politics and into the iron business.

His first political venture was in the state senate and then he went to Washington as a Representative in the Twenty-fourth and Twenty-fifth Congresses. He seems to have enjoyed politics, and he made friends with President Jackson, but his real love was in the Sussex hills, which he probably knew — in the eastern part of the County, at least — better than any other man before or since.

His vast knowledge of his home County came out of his passion for mineralogy, for he prowled the countryside with pick, shovel, and hammer. From Sparta across the York State line to Amity he looked at every rock. And of course, Providence had set him down in a rock hunter's paradise. Here, within a small radius of his home, he could find a diversity of specimens unequalled anywhere.

Dr. Sam found minerals that nobody had catalogued before, and he described them in scientific journals on both sides of the Atlantic. The ore that was to become of importance to his own iron industry he named **franklinite**. Others were later to be called **hardystonite, sussexite,** and — fittingly — **fowlerite.**

Dr. Fowler's forge at Franklin was called the "New Forge" because an ancient one had stood near as early as 1756. It closed down in 1776 (the owners were Tories) and remained unused for years. Then John Ford, who lived in Stockholm, reopened the mine with the idea of making iron from franklinite ore. He wasn't very successful, for he couldn't devise a system to keep up enough heat. Fowler went into the business with Ford, and finally bought him out, including works and mineral lands. By improving the methods of smelting, the doctor was able to make money at his forges, although he was never too successful in reducing franklinite. He knew what the trouble was: charcoal couldn't generate enough heat. He dreamed of the day when anthracite would be available and cheap enough to do the job.

By 1834, Franklin Furnace was on the map. Gordon's **Gazetteer** describes it: "... contains 2 forges of 2 fires each, a cupola furnace, a blast furnace not now in operation, a woolen manufactory for the manufacture of broad cloth, a grist and saw mill, a school house, and a new stone Baptist church, and 24 dwellings."

Fowler long preached the possibilities of zinc but seems to have given up hope of ever making anything out of his zinc holdings, for he had a shaky title to what was known as Mine Hill and never bothered to do anything about it. It was not until years after his death that zinc mining became of any importance to Franklin Furnace.

Young Sam Fowler, or Colonel Sam as they were to call the doctor's son later, was a vigorous personality in his own right. As a young man he studied law with Governor Haines, but he never practiced. He inherited his father's mines and furnaces and developed his holdings with energy and success. He also inherited his father's scientific bent and made some successful experiments with the use of zinc in paint. Then he went to New York, set himself up as a broker in mining stocks, and made a lot of money.

He was living in Port Jervis when President Lincoln called for 300,000 volunteers in 1862, but he came home to join up. Three companies of the 15th Regiment of N. J. Infantry were raised in Sussex County, and Samuel Fowler, young Sam, was appointed colonel.

But he was never to see active service and was invalided home. Despite his illness, Sussex County elected him to the Assembly which was to meet in January, 1865. When January came, he was much too ill to go, but he went. In Trenton he collapsed on the floor of the House and died in his hotel.

Sam's younger brother John, already in the army, transferred to his brother's regiment to serve in Company K with the Hardyston men he had grown up with. He was shot at Salem Heights in 1863, and his body was never found. There is a monument to him in North Church Cemetery, but his unmarked grave is somewhere in Virginia.

5. The 1830 Look

The story of the Fowlers has brought us to mention of the Civil War, but we're not quite ready to talk about that yet. Let's pause before we plunge ahead to take a look around us in and about the year 1830 and see what we had here.

The choice of 1830 for our inventory was determined by two considerations. It was the year of the first census after partition, for in 1824 Warren County had been set off from Sussex, and our County assumed the size and shape it now has. And, more important, Thomas Gordon's **Gazetteer** gives a detailed picture of the towns and hamlets of that time.

Andover in 1830 was near the bottom of a long decline. In 1845 Andover was to be revived when the iron mine opened again, but at this point it was still nearly dormant, as it had been since the mine had closed early in the century.

Branchville, on the other hand, can mark 1830 as the beginning of a period of rapid growth. In the next fifteen years the bustling little community was to acquire 4 stores, an academy, a church, 2 taverns, 3 grist mills, a dye plant, a carriage builder, 2 blacksmiths, a cooper, 32 dwellings, and about 200 inhabitants. How many people today know what a cooper did?

These statistics are taken from Barber and Howe's **Historical Collections** of 1845. But in 1830, Branchville, like Andover, was not yet of much importance.

Byram Township, however, was a different story. Says Gordon, "By the census of 1830 it contains 958 inhabitants, 187 taxables, 5 stores, 5 saw mills, 10 forge fires, 6 tan vats, 1 distillery, 123 horses and mules, 497 cattle over the age of 2 years." By 1845 the population was up to 1,153, but the forges had shrunk to 4.

Gordon thought that the Deckertown of 1830 owed its importance to the fact that it lay at the intersection of two turnpikes. He pictured it as containing "a grist mill, Presbyterian church, 4 stores, 2 taverns, and from 15 to 20 dwellings."

Frankford Township was booming as Gordon pictured it: "There was in the township in 1832, 6 stores, 14 run of stones, 2 carding machines, 460 horses and mules and 1,540 neat cattle, above 3 years old; 48 tan vats, 5 distilleries." The 1830 census reported a population of 1,996.

There was a Fredon postoffice in 1834, but it was not to be a township for another seventy years. But there was a "Greene" township, as Gordon called it. The whole township had a population of about 800, and 12 tan vats. Greendell was "Greenville," with 12 houses.

Hamburg, says the 1834 **Gazetteer,** "contains a church common to Baptists and Presbyterians, 2 taverns, 4 stores, 2 grist mills, and 15 or 20 dwellings. This is a thriving village, and the water power on the river offers strong inducements to settlers."

Hardyston was an important township in 1834, for it was not until 1845 that Sparta Township was created. Population totalled 2,588 by the 1830 census. Gordon lists all the usual distilleries and tan vats, and pays homage to "one of the most interesting mineral localities in the U. S." There were postoffices at Sparta, Monroe, and Harmonyvale; none at Franklin.

Lafayette was not a township in 1834 and the village of 10 or 12 dwellings also included a Baptist church, a tavern, a furnace, and a grist mill. The village was best known as a stage stop on the Union Turnpike.

Montague could boast about a thousand inhabitants in those 1830 days, and there were 6 stores and the inevitable distillery. Much of the economic life of the township centered upon the two turnpike roads which converged at the Delaware and crossed to Milford by the new bridge, built in 1826 at a cost of $20,000.

Newton was both township and small town at that time. The town, in Gordon's account, contained ". . . several streets, and a large common or public lot fronts the courthouse and prison. It contains about 130 dwellings and 900 inhabitants, 4 taverns, 8 extensive stores, 2 printing offices, a very large and commodious Presbyterian church, an Episcopal church and a Methodist church, 2 seminaries, in which the classics are taught, 6 common schools, 3 Sunday schools, a public library, a bank with a capital of $100,000, established in a handsome building, especially erected for it . . . There are in town 4 practicing attorneys, 4 physicians, and two resident clergymen. Some of the dwellings are very neat; the place has an air of business, and there is in fact a very considerable trade carried on with the surrounding country."

There seemed to have been some trouble about how to spell "Sandyston," for Gordon has it "Sandistone," while Barber and Howe make it "Sandiston." The "y" didn't get in until much later; or rather, didn't get back in, for it appears in some of the earliest uses of the word. Among other statistics the **Gazetteer** lists 4 merchants, 5 pairs of stones for grinding grain, 13 tan vats, and a distillery. The flat land between the Blue Mountain and the Delaware is singled out for its excellent crops of wheat.

I also notice, somewhat wistfully, that the population was about 1,000 people and that the total state, county, and local tax for the entire township was about $1,000. This assessment of about a dollar a head was pretty typical of the whole County in 1834!

Sparta village appealed to Gordon: "This is a very pleasant village, having some very good houses, a neat Presbyterian church with cupola, a schoolhouse, 2 grist mills, 2 saw mills, 4 forges for making iron, in which there are, together, 6 fires; 1 tavern, 3 stores, and from 30 to 40 dwellings."

But it is the 1845 **Historical Collections** that really beats the drum for "one of the most pleasant villages in this part of the state. The dwellings are neat, many of them ornamented with shade trees, and the surrounding scenery is of a bold and picturesque character."

Then the description breaks forth into lyrics: "Nature here wears some of her most bewitching charms, and enterprise is fast adding to the attractions of art. Within a brief period the village has doubled in size . . . One of the flour-mills is the largest in Sussex Co., and is the property of Mr. Morris, a citizen, and brother of the Mayor of New-York.

"Reader, when you would escape from 'Vanity Fair' to enjoy nature in her most luxuriant retirements, come to Sparta. It is one of her banqueting halls, where she keeps holiday the summer through. For the languid frame and the sick heart, there is nothing like the pure elastic air, the reviving atmosphere of these mountain solitudes, where every breeze visits the senses as if laden with the renovating spirit of life." Reader, when you would enjoy purple prose, read Barber and Howe!

We can hurry past Stanhope, described as a forge and about 30 dwellings, and Stillwater, both township and village, and in 1830 of little comparative importance. Nor do Vernon nor Walpack have much of interest for us in Gordon's description. About Wantage Township there is a little more. Its 1830 population was 4,034, with 11 storekeepers, 18 mills, 3 distilleries, post offices at Deckertown and Libertyville, 22 schools, 573 pupils, and 9 churches.

And that about completes the list. One hundred and thirty-five years ago we were a County of small hamlets, each nearly self-contained with its mills and tanneries, forges and stores, schools and churches. The farming was diversified, and each farmer produced pork, beef, leather, vegetables, fruit, and flour largely for his own use. When a depression came, or the land gave out, he loaded up his family, drove over to the Morris Turnpike, and headed for the West.

6. Newspapers and Newspapermen

In the days before the railroads, men read only the local papers, for a New York daily was expensive and late in arriving. So people bought the local weekly for two dollars a year. That was expensive too — two days' pay — which meant that a family subscribed to but one and depended upon it for most of its news and all of its opinions.

"News" would usually mean two solid columns of the President's budget message to Congress, or something of like profundity and indigestibility. Not until the 1860's did any local items creep in. Most of the paper was advertising, and all of it was pretty dull by our standards.

As far as we know, the County's first newspaper was first published January 8, 1796. Its proprietors were Elliott Hopkins and William Huston, and it was called the **Farmers' Journal and Newton Advertiser.** The compound title suggests a merger of two earlier papers, but there are no clues to support this idea. The paper made struggling appearances for about three years.

In 1813, John Hall began the Sussex **Register,** printed his first issue on July 6 in a building back of the Court House. He had a hard time of it for a number of years, but in 1835 Judge Hall (he held a fantastic number of different jobs in the community) employed Ben Edsall, gave him a free hand, and the paper began to prosper. By 1856 the **Register** was one of the leading rural weeklies in the country, and Edsall became a partner. The success of the **Register** is remarkable in a way, for it was a Whig paper run by two dauntless Whigs, and in those days this County was a fortress of Democracy. That the paper had a large circulation is a tribute to the esteem in which Hall and Edsall were held despite their politics.

Speaking of tribute, I too must acknowledge my tremendous debt to Benjamin B. Edsall. In 1853 the County celebrated the one hundredth anniversary of its establishment, and Edsall made the centennial address, which he later printed. It is a monumental piece of research from which I have borrowed heavily for the material on our early years. Most of what we now know about this County's early history was the result of Ben Edsall's digging out of the facts with tender loving care.

Meanwhile, in the fall of 1829, Colonel Grant Fitch had started to publish the New Jersey **Herald.** He had come to Newton some years before, had run a store that was a success and a cotton mill that wasn't, and began to publish the **Herald** in a building on the corner of Main and Spring streets.

The **Herald** had several editors in its early days, but finally in 1855 acquired Col. Morris Hamilton, a Princeton graduate and a lawyer. He was well-liked, and the paper grew substantially. He and Ben Edsall became bitter enemies, at least in the editorial columns, and their diatribes against each other make lively reading even today.

While these two were becoming firmly established, others were coming and going. The **Home Journal** was established in Sussex in 1849; the

Democrat came in 1853; papers called the Branchville **Record** and the Sussex **True Democrat** had brief existences. Copies of any of them would be collectors' items today. It was the Sussex **Independent**, first published in 1870, which was the next influential and enduring paper to enter the local weekly field. In 1885 George Keech began publishing the **Eagle** at Stanhope. Nor must we forget Charles E. Stickney's Wantage **Recorder**, published in Sussex beginning in 1894 and for nearly forty years.

7. The Civil War Begins

His name was Alex Stewart, he came from Green Township, and he was the first Sussex County boy to lose his life in the Civil War. He belonged to Company I of the Seventh N. J. Regiment, and there is irony in this, for Sussex men had enlisted in all the previous six regiments, and the Seventh was organized comparatively late.

The very first volunteers in the County were organized into Capt. James Fitts's "Union Volunteers" or Capt. Henry Ryerson's "Sussex Rifles." To Lincoln's call to arms the County responded promptly. To a mass meeting April 22, 1861, in the County park in Newton, came three thousand people from all over the area. Col. Sam Fowler of Franklin made the principal address. The Sussex Cornet Band played from an impromptu bandstand atop a wagon. Three thousand dollars was raised. After the meeting, Newton boys dragged Jeff Davis's effigy through the streets. Flags broke out all over.

Men poured in from all over the County to sign up with either the Fitts or the Ryerson outfits. They were lodged in the hotels; the local ladies began making their uniforms, and the volunteers began learning close order drill. On May 21, 1861, they left for the fighting. The Fitts company was now Co. D, Third N. J. Infantry, and Ryerson's had become Co. B of the Second.

The Second Regiment was to return three years and many battles later after suffering nearly seven hundred casualties. It fought at Gettysburg and Chancellorsville, but its day of glory came in September of '62, when it took the heights at Crampton's Gap with nothing but bayonets and courage. The Third Regiment's history is very similar, for both units belonged to the First N. J. Brigade, and were in most engagements together.

But it was the Fifteenth N. J. Volunteers that was closest to Sussex County hearts. It was full of our own, "Young Sam" Fowler was its colonel, and when the old Second reorganized, many of our soldiers there transferred to the Fifteenth. The regiment fought through the war in thirty-six battles, winning its highest honors in the Wilderness in May 1864. It was on May 12, 1864, that the Fifteenth suffered 150 casualties in a single half-hour's assault on the "Bloody Angle."

But while the Fifteenth claimed our first affection, it was the cavalry troopers who were the glamor boys. For years afterward, when County people talked of the exploits of local war heroes, they sooner or later got around to talking about Judson Kilpatrick of Deckertown and of the brilliant feats of his favorite Harris Light Cavalry (later the 2nd N. Y.) with two companies solid with Sussex recruits.

Hugh Judson Kilpatrick was born in Deckertown January 14, 1836. A cadet at West Point when war began, he was commissioned a second lieutenant before the school year was over, was promoted to captain three days later, and was wounded for the first time within a month. While recuperating, he learned of the organization of a new cavalry regiment, joined and was named lieutenant colonel, and hurried to Sussex County to enlist some of his old friends and neighbors.

Kilpatrick was soon colonel of the Harris Light, but he was not to lead it for long. When he was promoted to brigadier and later to major general, he was transferred to cavalry operations in the West, an assignment that led eventually to his commanding Sherman's horse soldiers on the march from Atlanta to the sea.

So distinguished a career as Kilpatrick's had to be rewarded, so after the war he was made the American minister to Chile. But he wanted to enter politics and felt that he should be cashing in on his brilliant record and reputation. So he came home to farm near Sussex, to earn quite a bit of money by going all over the country lecturing on his war experiences — he was an engaging speaker — and to try his hand at politicking.

But he was to be disappointed. Three times he was suggested for governor, but he never received the nomination. Once he ran for Congress, but Republicans stood no chance in this Democratic stronghold, even if they were war heroes.

In 1881 President Garfield sent him back to Chile. He was ill much of the time, and in June he died in far away Santiago. The Chilean girl he had wed sent his body home to lie at West Point.

He was our most distinguished soldier.

Chapter III
Making a Living and Having Fun

In this chapter we are going to be dealing largely with our economic life and with our recreation. And sometimes the two can't be kept apart, for Sussex County has depended on tourists and vacationists for part of its income ever since the turnpikes made it possible in the 1820's for city dwellers to escape to our lakes and hills.

We have already described the early iron industry in Chapter I and pictured its slow death around 1800. At that time we hinted that there was another chapter to the iron story, and that story we propose to tell now.

1. The Andover Mine and the One at Franklin

In 1845 shrewd old Peter Cooper founded the Trenton Iron Co. He picked his spot with care. He had an idea that he could use North Jersey's ore by having it floated to Trenton by the Morris Canal and the Delaware. He could use the Lehigh Canal to bring his anthracite. So he built what was to remain for twenty years the biggest iron works in the country. At Trenton he turned out the best quality of iron then being manufactured, and it was here that he pioneered the shift to steel.

Peter had a son-in-law, Abram S. Hewitt, who was even smarter than he. He was manager of the Trenton plant, and he was quick to see that the mushrooming rail roads (always two words then) were going to need vast quantities of rails to run on. Naturally, the firm which built the best rail would get the business. The first rails split with maddening frequency. Hewitt thought that he could make a rail that wouldn't split if only he could get ore good enough.

For months Abe Hewitt roamed the hills of New Jersey's northern counties, visiting forgotten forges and furnaces, testing and sampling. Finally, in 1847, he found what he wanted in the old mine hole in Andover. When Hewitt tested the iron in some fragments of pigs that lay hidden in the underbrush, his eyes shone. He held in his hands the whole railroad rail business of the United States.

Close-lipped and cagey, Hewitt played the role of the reluctant buyer and stole the mine for $2,500. He carted his ore to the Morris Canal and floated it to Phillipsburg, where he built the largest blast furnaces yet seen in America. The pig iron from these furnaces was shipped to Trenton, first by a canal down the Pennsylvania side of the Delaware, later by the railroad he got built down the New Jersey side. From his Andover ore Hewitt was able to make not only his rails but the first structural steel. In 1855, Nassau Hall, the historic center of Princeton University, was gutted by fire and rebuilt inside with Hewitt's railroad rails for I-beams. They are still there today.

During the Civil War Andover iron made rifle barrels, but by 1870 the Pennsylvania mills, with coal at their front doors, were gaining the edge in production. Sussex County's iron age was over, but the age of zinc was about to begin.

The period from 1850 to 1880, during which some zinc was mined, was more notable for prospecting and experimentation than for any great quantity of ore removed from the ground. Such ore as was mined was taken from Franklin to Lake Hopatcong by wagon, and thence by canal to Newark. French chemists had discovered that zinc oxide could replace white lead in paint, and the Newark smelting plant separated the ore by the French process. The by-products were important too: spiegel iron,

used to toughen railroad car wheels, and franklinite iron, which was so hard that it could be used as a lining for safes.

To attempt to trace the story of iron and zinc mining at Franklin from Fowler's successors (the Boston Franklinite Company) to the present New Jersey Zinc Company (the second of that name) is to get lost in a maze of claims, counterclaims, lawsuits, dissolutions, and reorganizations. The story is far too complicated for this history, but it has all been carefully recorded in Elwood Shuster's "Historical Notes of the Iron and Zinc Mining Industry in Sussex County, N. J."

One of the early problems which had baffled Fowler and those who followed him was the question of the mixed character of the ore. How

were they to separate economically the **franklinite** (which is iron, zinc, manganese, oxygen) from the **willemite** (silicate of zinc) and the zincite (red oxide of zinc)?

John Price Wetherill solved this one in 1888. He sucked the magnetic franklinite out of the mixture with an electromagnet. Many later refinements in magnetic separators didn't alter the basic principle. Wetherill's invention was a major breakthrough in the development of the zinc mining industry.

More dramatic was the problem of water, and this too had been largely solved before the New Jersey Zinc Co. was formed in 1891, most spectacularly at the Parker shaft of the Sterling Iron and Zinc Co. To overcome a torrent of water struck at the 580-foot level, which flooded the shaft in little more than a day, they pumped. It took fourteen months to pump back to the 580-foot mark. There they installed a big pump to handle the flow and went on down to 950 feet.

The stage was now set for really big developments in the zinc industry, but that story belongs to the twentieth century, and must wait for our next chapter.

2. The Agricultural Revolution

Our earliest farmers were not primarily interested in a cash crop. With transportation painfully difficult, they had to be self-sufficient, and what they produced was largely for their own use. Pork was more common than beef; it kept better. Likewise beans were popular because they could be stored, as could root vegetables. Cabbage would keep a while and could be made into sauerkraut. Some fruits were dried, but the staple fruit was the apple, which would keep in a cellar or cave, or could be made into vinegar or apple brandy.

There was always a sale for the extra hay and feed to horse owners in town, and the grist mill which ground a farmer's grain would often buy his surplus flour for shipment to the city. But many a Sussex County farmer lived comfortably almost exclusively on his own produce. Salt, tea, and dry goods (though his wife manufactured some of these) were about all he really needed from the store.

The turnpikes brought about the first farm revolution. And the railroads caused another. The Sussex County farmer who came into Newton or Deckertown on a shopping trip saw new items in the stores. And these items cost money. But the same wagons that brought in this merchandise stood waiting to carry our products for sale in the markets of the big cities to the southeast.

In no time at all our farmers became specialists, and the crops they concentrated on were hogs and butter. Before the railroads reached us in the 1850's, most of the County's production was picked up by commission merchants who carted it cityward by road, north to the railroad at Goshen, or south to the Morris Canal or the railroad at Morristown. Once the railroad reached Newton and Sussex (Deckertown then), those places became the shipping centers.

Some idea of the extent of the business done in those days, of its variety, may be obtained from this record of a single week's freight shipments from Newton in December, 1856: 1,047 hogs, 20 tons of butter, 4 tons of poultry, 2 tons of beef, 34 tons of flour, 3 carloads of new barrels and hoop poles. Today, of course, we import every one of those items (except the hoop poles!) and we have been doing so for many years.

The railroads could also transport cordwood and charcoal, and in the last half of the nineteenth century there was a considerable demand for both. It made a good winter job for the farmer, and every neighborhood had its rugged individualists who liked the independence of working by oneself and for oneself, and who made woodcutting or charcoal burning his way of life.

But the times changed. As the railroads which took our products to the city pushed further west, local hogs gave way to Kansas pork, local wheat was undersold by Minnesota and Dakota grain, local butter was replaced by butter from Wisconsin. Our local farmers had to find a new product to sell to the cities, and they had to find it quickly.

They found it in fluid milk, which could not be shipped from great distances. The first mention of a milk train appeared in 1858, and the first daily milk train started to run in 1863. It opened up a whole new era for Sussex County agricultural economy. But it was not a solution for everyone. Many who could not or would not make the change sold out and moved west. Emigration to Ohio had begun as early as 1788; it was considerable by 1817. In 1855 Iowa lands were advertised in the local papers. In 1856 a steady trickle of Sussex folk began moving to Kansas, Minnesota, Colorado. In the 1870's a group moved to Texas.

From 1830 to 1900 the population of the County remained steady, yet the towns grew. The only explanation is that the people were leaving the farms, and a steady decline in the price of farm land all during this period is further evidence.

41

But for those who stayed, milk was the salvation. It was never a totally acceptable salvation, however. Almost from the beginning the milk producers were beset by special problems.

By 1890, Sussex was deep in its part of an agricultural depression that affected the whole country. We cannot go into all the causes here, but we should note that another agricultural revolution was in progress. Many a local farmer condemned Congress, the railroads, and the "vested interests" because his milk sold for less than a dollar a hundred and his farm was worth but twenty dollars an acre. He never understood that the real villian was History. The early settlers had robbed the soil in scandalous fashion. When it played out, he had moved. Why put time and effort into rebuilding the land, when there was an endless supply of new, virgin land?

But the supply was no longer endless in 1890, so the farmer, tired of battling the milk buyers for a price to provide him a living, called in the auctioneer, took what he could get for what he had, and moved into Newton to work in the new shoe factory, or on to larger towns like Paterson and Newark, where he hoped there were larger opportunities.

For a time there was a hope that ice would become a bolster for the agricultural economy. It was strange that nobody had thought of it before. Ice-cutting was certainly no novelty to Sussex County farms. Rare indeed was the farm without an ice-house, and ice-cutting frolics had been a feature of the winter social season since earliest times. But as far as I can discover, a Philadelphia firm, the Knickerbocker Ice Co., built the first commercial ice house at White Lake in 1888. It was an imposing structure 265 feet long, 100 feet wide, and 32 feet high. It would hold 20,000 tons of ice. A year later another firm built a bigger one at Slater's Pond in Andover Township.

The big trick in harvesting an ice crop was in guessing when to cut. The thicker the ice the more desirable it was, and one could fill his ice house with less labor. But if one waited too long for the ice to grow thicker, one might run into a thaw and lose out. So there was always the agony of indecision for the man who had to give the word. It was almost a basic principle that the ice must be harvested by the first of February. After that the lengthening days and stronger suns cut quality even if the cold held out.

The Waterloo Ice Co. was the biggest operation around. E. C. Swift, of meat packing fame, was the president, and most of the output went to refrigerate Swift meats. Notable among the other ice companies was Brady's, which built what are now called Tamarack and Summit lakes in Hardyston Township.

But the weather turned capricious, and several open winters in the '90's caused a disappointing ice harvest. The ice business eventually moved on to places where there was a steadier, surer supply — the Poconos, for instance. It wasn't artificial ice or the mechanical refrigerator that prevented our County from becoming a great ice producer. It was those mild winters every now and then.

3. Famous Emigrants

We mentioned the people who were leaving the County because opportunities seemed better elsewhere, and perhaps this is a good point at which to stop and talk about some of those who made their mark in the world outside of Sussex County.

In 1827, John Bassett died in Natches, Miss., a peaceful printer who had seen stirring times, for he had gone out to Texas and played a prominent part in the revolt of 1824, when Mexico, of which Texas was a part, threw off the yoke of Spanish rule. So John Bassett, a Sussex County boy, has a small place in Texas history.

Some local young men went to the big city. Ely Moore, for instance, left the County and became a New York Congressman and a Whig leader. Suddenly he was arrested for defalcation to the extent of $18,500. Sussex County folks, who knew him best, said it just couldn't be, the charge was obviously Tammany Hall shenanigans. Moore proved his innocence, but his New York career was over, and he returned home and went into the newspaper business in Belvidere.

Here, too, his immense personal popularity was embarrassing to his political enemies. So, when he just missed election to the U. S. Senate by a few votes in 1851, they kicked him upstairs with an appointment as Indian Agent in the Nebraska Territory, which effectively removed him from the local political scene.

Of the many from Sussex County who invaded California in the mad days of the gold rush, Gabriel H. Post became the best known. As an early leading citizen of San Francisco, he was proposed by the citizens of that city for the state senate. He turned them down. Too much engrossed with business, he said. What he meant was that he was making too much money. The strain was too great. He was only forty when he died in 1861, much mourned by the folks by the Golden Gate for his "great public spirit and abounding generosity."

About John Cleves Symmes we wrote at some length in Chapter I. We labelled him Sussex County's leading figure in the Revolution, and we speculated how, with a little luck, Symmes might have been our most famous emigrant.

But it was not to be, and Symmes died nearly forgotten. The little caravan from Walpack which he led to the Ohio was to produce two famous figures by descent. The first, whose story we have already referred to,

43

was Symmes's daughter, who became the wife of President William Henry Harrison. The other famous descendant of Sussex County forebears had to wait longer for national recognition. But when, in 1863, the eyes of America turned to Tennessee, where the fighting at Lookout Mountain and at Chickamauga was the topic of consuming interest, the name of General W. S. Rosecrance (as he spelled it) was in the headlines of every paper in the North for many days. The general was the son of Jacob Rosenkrans, who had gone with Symmes to the Ohio country from Walpack, many years before. Later the general was to serve as an ambassador and as a U. S. Senator from California.

Two local boys who struck it rich in the big city were John Haggerty and "Doctor" David Jayne. John Haggerty was born at Augusta, probably in 1773. Just when he left the County I do not know, nor is it clear just when he began as an auctioneer in Manhattan, but he became the most famous hammer-wielder of his time. He lived to be ninety and died at Whitestone, near where the great bridge now touches Long Island. He was the perfect prototype of an Alger hero.

Dr. David Jayne—I am almost certain that the medical degree was self-conferred—was born in Byram Township in the early nineteenth century. Inventing a patent medicine cure-all, he went to Philadelphia and parlayed his concoction into a million dollars. Surprisingly, many quack preparations like Jayne's had large bands of loyal users. The secret of his devotion was often a large helping of alcohol in the formula, which enabled nice old ladies who had taken the pledge to achieve a warm inner glow without any pricking of conscience. David Jayne, the Sussex County boy, was the elderly ladies' friend. In his later years (he died in 1866), he spent freely of his large fortune on various philanthropies. Do you suppose his conscience pricked him?

Mine would bother me if I claimed Benjamin Lundy for Sussex County, and yet I wish I could. He was born at Allamuchy January 4, 1789, and that was Sussex County then, and a Quaker settlement. But Lundy left us early, to grow into a leading abolitionist editor and associate of William Lloyd Garrison. The Lundys were a widespread family; some of them went to Canada at an early day. Here, in the War of 1812, was fought the Battle of Lundy's Lane. Its importance may have been minimized in the history book you studied, for the American's didn't win it. But it is interesting to record that the Lundys of Lundy's Lane were a branch of the Lundys of Sussex County.

We have already made mention of the fact that Governor Daniel Haines was, in his later years, practically a Newark exile from the home of his youth, but he was not the only lawyer who left looking for bigger opportunity. After the Civil War we lost Thomas McCarter, who became not only a great Newark lawyer but the rock on which grew the great Public Service Corporation. Next time you travel over the McCarter Highway, remember that its name has Sussex County origins.

Two of our most famous emigrants never completely cut their ties with home. One of these was Henry C. Kelsey, and another was John W. Griggs. Kelsey always remained a director of the old Sussex National Bank (which later merged with the Merchants), and he is buried in the Newton cemetery. Griggs deserted us more completely, but he always maintained a sentimental attachment to the Sussex hills.

Kelsey left the County in 1870 to be N. J. Secretary of State and a power in state politics. At Trenton he built such a reputation for skill in the devious processes of politicking that one reputable historian was led to claim quite seriously that he feigned deafness, in order to hear conversations he was not supposed to hear!

For twenty-seven years the Kelsey faction dominated New Jersey politics under a succession of Democratic governors. It is a curious item of state history that when people tired of unending Democratic domination, they selected as governor John W. Griggs, who was living in Paterson when he was elected, but who was Sussex County born and bred. Griggs's election in 1895 started a fifteen-year Republican dynasty that was to endure until Woodrow Wilson brought success to the Democrats again.

Griggs's term as governor was short. His good friend Garret Hobart was Vice President and used his influence to have Griggs appointed Attorney General. The crowning achievement of Griggs's career was his designation as an American member of the World Court at the Hague in 1901.

John W. Griggs died in 1927, full of years and honors. One of his last recorded speeches was delivered at the dedication of the Historical Building in Newton. It was a graceful reminiscence of early days. Every line of it reveals that John W. Griggs, Governor, Cabinet member, international judge, was still deeply in love with the County where he first saw the light of day.

4. The Railroads Dominate Our Living

So far this chapter has mentioned the railroads many times, and this is inevitable, for from the Civil War until World War I the railroad played nearly as important a part in our daily lives as the automobile does today.

As early as 1836 the citizens of Deckertown (Sussex) were thinking in terms of a railroad that would link the Hudson and the Delaware across the County. But except for some surveying of possible routes, nothing was done. The main activity in railroad building was by the Erie just

45

to the north of us at Chester and Goshen, and by the Morris and Essex, later the Lackawanna, which had reached Morristown to the south of us. For years it remained doubtful in which direction our own railroad outlet would lead us.

The question was partially answered when Cooper and Hewitt re-opened the Andover iron mines in 1847. They built the Sussex Mine Railroad to transport their ore southward to the canal and to connect with the Morris and Essex. Of its extension to Newton we have already told.

In the days after the Civil War, the biggest railroad news was made by the New Jersey Midland R. R. Organized in 1869, the company set speed records that open our eyes even today. The Midland built a road and ran its first train from Newton to Sussex in June, 1871. On the Fourth of July, same year, it opened its Franklin-Unionville section, and six months later had pushed to Newfoundland over the route we now know as the Susquehanna. Ten years later an extension from Ogdensburg was built southwestward through Swartswood and Stillwater and on to Strouds-burg and the coal fields.

The early 1870's is also the time when the Lehigh and Hudson built from Belvidere to run through the County from Tranquility and Andover to Franklin and Vernon and on to join the Erie at Greycourt, N. Y. And what became the Lehigh and New England roughly paralleled this route, crossing the County from southwest to northeast and touching Swarts-wood Junction, Augusta, and Sussex. The early dreams of the builders of this road are revealed by one of its early names, "The Pennsylvania, Poughkeepsie, and Boston R. R." Indeed, there was a time in 1891 when a through train ran over the L. & N. E. tracks from Washington, D. C., to Boston.

By 1890, the great period of railroad building in our area was over. Only the Lackawanna cut-off, constructed in 1910, and crossing the County from Lake Hopatcong just below Andover to Greendell and Blairstown, remained as a major building project. The rapid railroad expansion in the County was typical of what was going on all over the country, and right in the center of the mushrooming rail activity was John I. Blair, one of the most remarkable citizens we have yet produced, and certainly the richest.

He was born at Foul Rift on the Delaware in 1802, but he grew up in Hope. Both of these points were in Sussex County then, which is why we can claim him. He was fifty-eight years old and already successful in business when he went to the Republican national convention in Chicago in 1860 (it nominated Lincoln) and became excited by the opportunities for railway expansion in the West and Middle West. From his efforts came the Union Pacific, and eventually he owned a piece of twenty different railroad companies.

Self-educated himself, Blair was interested in education and contributed largely to Princeton, Lafayette, and to Grinnell College in Iowa. In 1849 he became interested in Blair Academy and gave liberally to that school as well as to other projects in the town he had chosen as his home. So generous was he that the town decided to change its name from Gravel Hill to Blairstown.

In 1868, John I. Blair was the Republican nominee for governor. But the Democrats swept the state, even though the great Horace Greely came from New York to make speeches for him. Blair lived to be ninety-seven, surviving his wife and all but one of his children, and dying December 2, 1899.

John Insley Blair, who had just missed being born into the eighteenth century, did not quite live to see the twentieth.

5. Sports And Recreations

From very early days Sussex County has been a vacationland, and entertaining summer visitors has been a considerable industry from long before the days of the automobile, or, for that matter, of the railroad. In an earlier chapter we gave you one visitor's enthusiastic comments on Sparta as a vacation spot in 1845, and by that time many communities in the County had a loyal band of "city people" who returned year after year to this or that hotel. And many a farmer's wife augmented her egg money by taking in a few summer boarders who were drawn by farm-size meals, feather ticks, and the smell of new-mown hay.

It is impossible to get any idea of the actual number of summer visitors we attracted then. But in a curious way we can tell that it was considerable, especially after the Civil War, and the curious way is this: a grim little news item, with changing names of people and places, but otherwise identical, kept appearing week after week: "Miss Joanne Bertram of Brooklyn, drowned while bathing in Lake Hopatcong on Tuesday last."

Train excursions brought a great many folks to the County on one-day trips — Cranberry Lake was a favorite terminal for these. One excursion to Newton in 1868, planned to bring a lot of Grant clubs from Newark for a gigantic parade and rally, got so involved in a series of minor accidents and tie-ups that the train never arrived until 11 p. m. But they paraded anyway, were fed by the local Republican ladies, and re-embarked at three in the morning. I wonder if they were still for Grant?

But local folks not only helped visitors have fun; they succeeded in having their share, too. Excursions out of the County were just as popular as incoming ones. Long Branch was one favorite objective, Far Rockaway another. The train would leave at 5:45 a. m. or thereabouts and bring home the weary excursionists late in the evening.

Another frequent visiting-point for local one-day excursions was Central Park in New York City. Once, in 1869, the train took nine carloads of Sussex Countyites to Hoboken, where they took a boat to 55th Street. On the return trip the boat took them on a detour down the bay before returning them to the Hoboken dock, where the train had them back in Newton by 10:30 p. m. Round trip, $2.50.

And then there was baseball. The first game in the County was played August 30, 1865, on the field of Mount Retirement Seminary near Sussex, between the school team and the Delawares of Port Jervis. The score was 36-14 in favor of the school. Five days earlier the two teams had played at Port Jervis, the Delawares winning that time.

One year later, 1866, with the soldiers home from the war, there were baseball teams everywhere. Newton had its Eurekas and Stars. Every game generated such great excitement that notices were printed pleading, "All persons not playing in the game will please not dispute with the umpire, as it tends to create dissatisfaction between the players." The big game of 1866 in Newton brought the Nationals of Morristown, with a New Jersey ex-governor pitching, but the Stars set them down, 30 to 22.

By the turn of the century scores were down to the levels always associated with the days before the lively ball. Newton and Branchville emerged as the great rivals. The interest was intense and all but unanimous. When Newton played at Branchville, for instance, Newton merchants closed their stores on the afternoon of the game and everybody went. Today some of the names in the box scores look vaguely familiar to an old baseball fan, and they are; both sides hired as many professional ball players as their pocketbooks would permit. On two occasions the peerless Hal Chase performed for Branchville.

Fishing was always popular in our County, with bass and trout fisherman getting most of the attention. From very early years fishermen from the city would come to local streams and lakes to try their luck. The May, 1893, issue of **The American Angler** says, "The angler can find in the lakes in the hills of N. J. (the author had just visited Deckertown) excellent fishing for black bass, pickerel, and trout . . . **Here black bass may be taken of a weight that the angler will admit to be rare. Here trout were taken this spring that fairly rival the Adirondack trout in size and far surpass them in brilliancy of sheen and delicacy of form."**

The Delaware and Walkill both produced fine bass, and some notable pickerel came from Swartswood Lake in those days. A curious sidelight is that in 1878 an attempt had been made to stock the Delaware with salmon. But nothing ever came of it.

However, for many the real highlight of the recreation season in the County was the Farmers' Picnic. Many of our older residents still remember it fondly, and to most of those it means the one held annually for many years at Lake Grinnell. This was the first, the biggest, and it endured the longest. But there were other people for whom "farmers' picnic" meant the annual shindig at Culver's Lake, which was neither so big nor so famous.

The first picnic at Lake Grinnell was held in 1882, and within a few years the affair was drawing six thousand people by special train or horse and wagon from Sussex, Branchville, Newton, and Franklin. After a morning spent in visiting, the picnic dinner came out of the big hampers— fried chicken, ham, baked beans, potato salad, pickles of all kinds, ice cream, cake, pie. There were lots of incidentals to fill in the chinks. Seventy years ago good knife-and-fork men approached the table without a thought of calories or cholesterol.

About 2 p.m. the speaking began. Oratory was a part of life for our grandsires, and any speech under sixty minutes was dismissed as just a few ex tempore remarks. The Congressman would be there, and all the local office-holders and aspirants. When the speeches were over, everybody turned to fun. Business had already been brisk at the concessions; now it turned feverish. Most of them — merry-go-round, ice cream, shooting gallery, etc. — were operated by local people who bid for the locations. Then there was a dance pavilion, a freak show, photographers.

But milking time came all too soon, and while there were fireworks in the evening sometimes, the crowd dwindled pretty rapidly late in the afternoon.

One other favorite sport remains to be mentioned — horse racing. The first horse races in Sussex County were at Deckertown in 1814 between runners, but as roads improved, harness horse interest took over. The County produced one fabulous trotter, Goldsmith Maid, and countless minor speedsters. Every town had its track, but any straight stretch of road could produce a "brush" when a couple of fanciers of horse-flesh — and who wasn't, then? — would meet up on the way to town and decide to try each other out.

A famous race here during the Civil War matched a Monmouth County horse, George B. McClellan, against a N. Y. state champion called Elmira Pet. But it was the next year, 1862, that produced one of the most amazing horse exhibitions ever seen locally. It came about as the result of a bet between Jacob B. Konkle of Newton, and a man named Snyder from Newark. To win a wager of $100, Konkle set out to trot his five-year-old horse ninety-six miles inside of twelve hours. He did it. The plucky little trotter made a record of ninety-seven and one-third miles in eleven hours! But Snyder welshed on his bet, claiming chicanery. Konkle (he was operating the Cochran House at the time) had hitched his horse in a team with a succession of fresh horses, which pulled most of the load. Offsetting this assistance was the fact that the super-marathon was held on a rough and frozen track in cold December weather.

Our ancestors, movieless, televisionless, autoless, still had a lot of fun.

Chapter IV
Only Yesterday

On June 8, 1903, Sussex County was one hundred and fifty years of age. For nearly a year men planned for the sesqui-centennial, and they knew right from the start what they hoped to achieve. They were out to beat the record set by the centennial celebration in 1853, and they had their work cut out for them. That had been a tremendous affair with parades, speeches, dinners, and general jollification that many of the older folks could look back upon as the biggest day of their lives.

The high point of the one hundredth anniversary had been the historical address prepared and delivered by Benjamin Edsall, to whose research I have already acknowledged my indebtedness. Edsall's 1853 speech took three hours (after two hours there was a fifteen-minute intermission for the recuperation of speaker and listeners), and he seems to have held their interest all the way. Today it is hard for us to imagine listening for three hours to anybody speaking on anything!

Since they wanted to top the centennial, the first move of the 1903 planners was to find a worthy successor to Edsall to write and deliver the address at the one-and-a-half century mark. They found him in Francis J. Swayze, brilliant young Newton attorney newly appointed judge, who set to work immediately to collect his material.

Swayze's speech followed Edsall's for the material down to 1853, then made use of the files of the Sussex **Register** (later merged with The New Jersey **Herald)** to fill in the succeeding fifty years. His job was a difficult one, for this County's history from the Civil War to 1903 is anything but spectacular. Mostly we were marking time, and the progress we made, while solid, was slow and furnished little opportunity for engag-

ing narrative. But I am indebted to Judge Swayze for considerable material in this history, and I must pay envious tribute to his polished literary style.

The Sesqui-Centennial Celebration, which was attended by about 15,000 people, and at which Judge Swayze read his address, was held September 2, 1903. It was an important day in the County, for it marked far more than just a century and a half of the County's official existence. I do not believe Swayze or the others there realized all of what was happening, but the old way of life was changing. Regardless of the calendar, the twentieth century may be said to begin in Sussex County on September 2, 1903.

1. Industrial Development

The early years of the twentieth century saw the mining industry of the Franklin-Ogdensburg area finally reach its peak. We have already described how the invention of the Wetherill separator permitted a great forward step in the local industry. Equally important as a milestone of progress was the formation of the modern New Jersey Zinc Company in 1897.

This move brought the entire ore body under single undisputed ownership for the first time. The new company also acquired the smelting plants of the four merging companies, located at Jersey City, Newark, and Bethlehem, Penna., as well as zinc mines in several other states.

In 1910 the Palmer shaft was put into operation after four years of preparation, and the old Parker shaft, which for twenty years had produced the bulk of the ore mined, was closed. In 1912 the N. J. Zinc Co. took over the operations of the Sterling Hill mine. Some idea of the success of the project can be understood from the population figures. In the thirty years following 1895, "Franklin Furnace" increased its population by nine hundred per cent. The modern borough of Franklin dates from its corporation in 1913.

Meanwhile industry was invading other parts of the County. Small textile manufactories — mostly woolens or silk — had existed among us from very early days, but they employed only a few hands, were often seasonal, and did little to give us the industrial look. The first mill which hired a considerable work force and gave its community the look and something of the attitude of an industrial town was the H. W. Merriam Shoe Company, which turned out its first pair of shoes in Newton in June, 1873. The business began modestly with fifty employees and grew until forty years later it was employing 550 and was the biggest plant making shoes in New Jersey.

There were other plants, too, in the beginning years of the twentieth century. In Hamburg the Union Waxed and Parchment Paper Company was providing jobs for about 200 in the early decades. But most of the others were small in pre-World War I days and did little to modify the predominantly rural picture which the County had maintained since the decline of the forges and furnaces in the early 1800's.

2. New Ideas In Farming

We have told the story of how our farmers made the transition from hogs and butter to milk, and we tried to hint that this new way of life for Sussex County farms was not entirely satisfactory, that the price of farms still fell, and that the exodus from the farm to the towns and cities, or to the West, still continued throughout the nineteenth century. But now let us look for a little at the farmers who stayed with the dairy business and describe how they met and solved their problems.

One of the earliest attempts at helping the dairy farmer with his difficulties had been the Five States Milk Producers' Union. I am going into its short career with a little detail here, for the problem which brought it about is still with us, and the solution it attempted has been tried on other occasions. Its unhappy history has been repeated many times in many places. The union was born of desperation in 1890, when milk was bringing sixty cents for a forty-quart can, and farms were selling at twenty dollars an acre, buildings included. When there were buyers, that is.

Suddenly, like asparagus in May, locals of the Union were springing up all over, one at each railroad shipping point. Hamburg had the first one, followed by others at Sussex, Monroe, Lafayette, House's Corner, Newton, and many more.

Leading spirit of the farm protest was Lewis J. Martin of Sussex. Forty-six years old in 1890, he was well qualified for leadership. As a young attorney he had filled in as County Clerk when his father had become ill in that office, had served in the legislature, been a county judge, and was director of the Farmers' National Bank.

As Martin saw it in 1890, the problem was three-fold: the Milk Exchange had complete control of the price, discriminatory freight rates let in cheap Western milk to undersell the local product, and the Exchange had so long been diluting thirty quarts of whole milk with ten quarts of skimmed milk that milk was considered a dishonest product, the housewives rejected it, and the whole great metropolitan area used but 16,000 cans a day.

To remedy the condition, Martin proposed:

1.   That the milk producers set up their own creameries. Milk would still be sold to the Exchange, but at the Union's price, and enough would be held back and processed into butter and cheese at the union-operated creameries to keep the price up.

2.   A new law would be pushed through the legislature abolishing the discriminatory freight rates. Known as the Bale Bill for the Sussex County Assemblyman who sponsored it, it was written by Lewis J. Martin.

Would the farmers stick together? That was the question to which nobody had the answer, but the union's supporters were heartened by what happened in Branchville in mid-February, 1890. When the Milk Exchange agent appeared to sign up the dairymen for another year, the Branchville producers stood solid for the union, and not a signature did he get.

Meanwhile the Bale Bill had sailed through the Assembly, but ran into trouble in the Senate. And, as April 1, 1890, approached, the list of farm sales grew longer and longer. The Inslee herd of Jerseys, some of the finest animals in the country, were sold at auction. Jerseys were highly favored in the County then, much more so than either Holsteins or Guernseys. Most herds were overwhelmingly grade cows, but every farmer wanted a few Jerseys to keep his butterfat average up. Yet that superlative herd brought an average of but $85. Top price was $151 — for one of the finest Jersey cows on this side of the Atlantic.

Suddenly there was trouble. Up in Orange County, N. Y., a despairing local threw in the sponge when it became clear to them that New York City was flooded with milk for which there was no sale. Then, a creamery in Sussex failed, and confidence in the ability of the Milk Producers' Union to run its own creamery business was shaken. At this psychological moment the Milk Exchange offered a deal. Not only would they give the farmers a chance to buy a big block of the corporation's stock at par, they would appoint an executive committee to fix the price of milk, and on this committee the farmers would have a majority of one. Though the Union's leaders warned that this was the same old wolf in very transparent sheep's clothing, the shaken rank and file voted to leave the offer "open for further consideration."

But the decisive stroke was the defeat of the Bale Bill. When the committee to which the bill had been assigned refused to report it out, our state senator, Peter B. Smith, got a resolution before the senate instructing the committee to bring in the bill, which would provide lower freight rates for New Jersey milk. But despite Smith's feverish dedication to the cause, the senate voted 11-10 not to bring in the bill.

The Five States Milk Producers' Union was dead as of that moment. The great fight was over four months after it had started. A magnificent effort at having the farmers work together had failed.

It was not the end of farmers' organizations or of attempts to better their lot by helpful legislation. What the failure of the Five States Union did accomplish was to turn the dairymen to looking for other methods to improve their economic position. It was after this date that farmers began to realize that economic survival was going to depend on their producing better milk and producing it more cheaply. And thus began the great era of agricultural education that was to make all the difference for the prosperity of Sussex County farms.

Not that the education of farmers was an entirely new idea. Certainly local farm people, like their colleagues everywhere, had been educating themselves informally for a long time through their agricultural fairs.

The first fair in Sussex County was held November 7 and 8, 1821. The account is interesting enough and reveals enough about the state of agriculture in this region to be described at some length. Here is the story from the Sussex **Register,** in those days the only paper in the County, which still included Warren:

"Each day was ushered in by the ringing of a bell and the hoisting of a flag. Members met at the house of Nathan Drake at 9 a. m. Articles of domestic manufacture were exhibited at the Courthouse. At 3 p. m. an auctioneer sold all stock that owners wished to dispose of. On the second day, exercises were held in the Presbyterian church at 10 a. m. Members of the Society wore three ears of wheat in the left side of their hats. Dinner was served at Nathan Drake's, and premiums were paid in cash immediately after dinner.

"The first day was very stormy, but the attendance was respectable. The prizes were as follows: Best stallion, Benj. F. Hunt, Oxford, $15; best three-year-old colt, Robert Goble, Hardwick, $10; best bull not over 3 years, Nathan A. Shaver, Stillwater, $10; best milch cow, Walter L. Shee, Hamburg, $10; best pair fatted oxen, Nicholas Ryerson, Vernon, $15; best pair working oxen, Robert A. Linn, Hamburg, $10; best yearling calf, Walter L. Shee, $8; best ram, John VanDeren, Newton, $5; best ewe, James VanSickle, Newton, $5; best ten wethers, William Darrah, $10; best boar and best sow, James VanSickle, each $5; best firkin of butter made between May 1 and June 15, Joseph Northrup, Newton, $8; best piece of woolen cloth (10 yards), the Misses Margaret and Elizabeth Shafer, Stillwater, $8; exhibits of dressed flannel made by the family of John Lanterman, Hardyston, and a piece of linen made by Mrs. Elizabeth Ryerson, Frankford, did not come within the rules of the society, but were favorably noticed; Robert A. Linn, Hamburg, received a premium of $15 for best three acres of wheat, having an average of 35½ bushels to the acre. The variety was called Benedict. Mr. Shee stood second with the same variety. Walter L. Shee received $10 for best three acres of corn — a total of 305 bushels of ears, and expected his planting of fourteen acres to average 100 bushels an acre.

"Issac Dennis, of Hardwick, raised 412 bushels of potatoes on one acre and five rods of ground, and received a premium of $5. After payment of premiums, Judge Robeson declined re-election as president. and he was succeeded by Walter L. Shee. The Board of Directors consisted of thirty persons."

The fair continued for a time, but seemed to die with the division of the County in 1824. It was 1857 before another attempt was made, and this new organization held an annual fair right through the Civil War, but interest died soon after and the fair finally closed down in the late 1860's. But interest never fully died, and after short-lived attempts in the 1880's and 1920's a permanent organization was effected in 1940 when the Sussex County Farm and Horse Show Association was formed. The first show was held on Thursday, Friday, and Saturday of the second week in August, 1940, on the same grounds where it has been held ever since. The show in 1941 was an even bigger success than the first venture, but then war interrupted, and no shows were held from 1942 through 1945. The three-day show was resumed in 1946, lengthened to four days in 1947, to five days in 1950, and to six days in 1963.

However, the first real attempt at formal agricultural education came just before the turn of the century, when the legislature set up a Farmers' Institute in each county having an agricultural society. These were yearly affairs with speakers from the colleges or from among outstanding farmers of this and other states. Their success was at best partial, and it was 1912 before a real effective program of education began with the establishment of the Sussex County Board of Agriculture, the second such organization in the United States. First financed largely by the Lackawanna Railroad, it began to receive state and federal funds in 1913, and later, annual county appropriations.

The first official act of the County Board in 1912 was to appoint H. W. Gilbertson as County Agricultural Agent, although he had a different title then. One of the first such agents in the country, it was Gilbertson's job to bring to the farmers the results of the agricultural experimentation that had been going on for years in the colleges, but which the men on the farms had had small chance to find out about. Gilbertson went to work immediately demonstrating the then new commercial fertilizers and initiating brand new cow-testing programs.

By 1917 a Home Demonstrator was needed to help with programs for women and clubs. In 1919 the first high school agriculture course began at Newton, followed in three years by the course at Sussex. And in 1928 the 4-H Clubs needed their first county 4-H leader.

Over the years there have been many other developments and innovations—the County Board of Vocational Education, the County Vocational School of Agriculture, the Cooperative Breeding Association, the Grange, the Dairymen's League, the Cooperative Dairy Sales Association, the Holstein-Friesian Association, the United Milk Producers. All of these, and many others not mentioned, have contributed at some time or another and in some way or another to helping Sussex County farmers to do the job more efficiently.

3. The Growth of Institutions

If industry and agriculture were growing in the early days of this century, the institutions — schools, banks, and churches — were keeping pace. The schools, in fact, were already on the move by that September day in 1903 which we have selected as the opening of our modern era. They have been for nearly a year. Modern education with us can be dated from October 7, 1902, when Ralph Decker was appointed to succeed Luther Hill as county superintendent.

At one time there were 120 schools in the County. When Mr. Decker became superintendent, there were still 98, and 88 of these were one-room schools. Some of them had names like Wolf Pit, Blooming Grove, Cherry Ridge, East Mountain, Mt. Benevolence, Brick House, Statesville, Plains, Brooklyn, and Germany Flats. Today the one-room school is gone, and, sentiment and colorful names notwithstanding, it's a good thing, too.

At the turn of the century, Newton was the only community with a high school. Now all students live within reach of one of four modern public high schools and a parochial high school, all equipped to give college preparatory or various types of vocational training.

Perhaps Ralph Decker's greatest strength as the guide of our school's growth was his instinct for good public relations. His own account of how he organized the campaign for consolidating one-room schools is told in his monograph, "Then and Now: Forty Years in the Schools of Sussex County." He writes:

"Realizing that we could go no faster than public opinion would allow us, we determined to go to our people with a program of education.

"We took pictures of actual conditions, had slides made, procured a stereopticon operated by acetylene gas and toured the county. Crowds came to our meetings, and thus was laid the foundation for our future **work in consolidation."**

When the time to educate the citizens to the need for school programs in athletics, health, music, art, and manual training, and the time to sell them on 4-H and extension programs arrived together, Mr. Decker and the County's teachers organized "Get-Together Day." The title implied cooperation between farms and schools. It was an all-day affair with kids and adults — sometimes 6,000 — coming together at Franklin. There were exhibits of school work, cattle, farm machinery. A track and field meet in the morning was followed by an afternoon pageant.

Eventually the day was discontinued, but before it passed from the scene, music, athletics, and art were established in the school curriculum, **and the 4-H and extension programs were booming.** Get-Together Day **had served its purpose.**

We have made little mention of Sussex County's churches since our earliest days, when we told of the origins of the Reformed congregations in the Minisink settlements and mentioned some of the early pastors who were also schoolmasters.

The various denominations arrived in the County as parts of the different waves of immigration. First were the Dutch with their Reformed denominations, followed by the Germans with the Moravian settlement at Hope, then the English ironmasters, who brought the first Episcopal church to the County at Newton in 1769, and the Presbyterian church about 1780.

The first Methodist church dates from 1787 at Frankford Plains, though an early Reformed church had been located there for many years.

The Reverend Richard Bolger said mass at Newton on November 25, 1821, for the first Catholic service in the County, but this was missionary territory for the Catholics until 1854, when the whole County was made a single parish and a first church built in Newton.

A Baptist church with eight members was located at Augusta in 1756; the Christian denomination, first at Branchville in 1826, moved to Baleville in 1830; the Congregationalists seem to have been at Beemerville as early as 1744. These Congregationalists came from New England in a body, and one of the early pastors was the Rev. Jabez Collver, who owned a big tract of land in "Collver's Gap" and near Culver's (as we spell it today) Lake. He was a full-fledged Tory and emigrated to Canada after the Revolution. The congregation was finally absorbed by the Presbyterians.

Then, in the years before the Civil War, as the population stabilized, new churches grew less common, and few more congregations were organized down until the present day. Some church buildings outlived their congregations, as witness the early Reformed churches which were deserted or replaced by Presbyterians and Methodists. Some churches followed the population shifts, as witness the division of the Sparta church to make the North Church, and the removal finally of the Presbyterians from North Church to Hamburg.

Now, in recent years, with the population increasing again, we have new denominations appearing, as witness the Lutherans at Newton and Sparta, the Assembly of God at Hamburg, Christian Scientists at Sparta and Newton, Jehovah's Witnesses, Wesleyan Methodists, and the Jewish Center.

Banking began in Sussex County in 1818 with the establishment of the Sussex Bank, and this proved adequate for all of our financial needs until 1849, when the Farmers' Bank of Wantage opened for business. The newspapers of the period tell a story of counterfeit bank notes of the Farmers' Bank being picked up in Newton several days before the bank had opened in Sussex!

Following the organization of the Merchants' National Bank in 1864 (the other two banks became national banks about this time) there was a lull in the foundation of new banking institutions for nearly fifty years. Then the upswing of economic activity in the County brought about the founding of the Newton Trust Company in 1902, the bank at Branchville in 1904, the Hardyston Bank at Hamburg in 1906, and the Sussex County Trust Company at Franklin in 1919.

The merger of the Sussex Bank and the Merchants' in 1925 brought this particular era of banking to a close. At the present day we are seeing a new phase of the evolution of banking among us — the springing up of branches of these parent banks in many locations throughout the County.

In an odd sort of way, the merger of the Sussex with the Merchants' marked the close of another era as well. The last meeting of the directors of the Sussex Bank prior to merger was held December 30, 1924. One of the directors was not there. Despite his ninety years, he had planned to attend; in fact, he had missed few meetings in the many years of his directorship. But he had died that afternoon, on the very eve of the merger for which he had labored mightily.

His name was Luther Hill, and he was the last of the County's giants. We do not produce men like that nowadays. We have superior men among us, to be sure, but they are all specialists. They are prominent farmers, or engineers, or merchants. The men of Hill's stripe — men like Daniel Haines, Martin Ryerson, Ben Edsall — were restive without a finger in a dozen pies. Their lives followed a pattern. Almost all went to work at an early age, usually in a store. Almost all had more education than was common, preferably under Dunn at Newton, Rankin at Sussex, or Stiles in Wantage. A surprising number took a try at school teaching early in their careers; Luther Hill stayed with it longer than most. Many of them were bank directors, and most of them flirted with politics at one time or another. Almost to a man they were stalwart supporters of some church.

Luther Hill, who died in 1924, was born March 9, 1834. What a span! He is a connecting link for our whole history, for in his boyhood he knew some of the real pioneers. Yet many are alive in our own day who remember him well.

He was born in Green Township, eighth of the nine children of Samuel and Elsie Hill. At a very early age — probably about twelve — he went to work for Samuel Hunt of Huntsville in Hunt's store.

This was the most important event in young Luther's life, for Samuel Hunt was himself one of the "giants" and his influence on the boy was profound. It was from Hunt that he learned farming, Democratic politics, a love for books, and a passion for local history.

From Hunt's farm he went to Mt. Retirement Seminary, about 1850, to study under Edward A. Stiles. For more than forty years, first as founder and director of his private school and then as county superintendent, Stiles devoted himself to the education of the youth of our section, and the degree of his success can be measured by the large numbers of important citizens who were alumni of his classes.

Then came a period when young Luther Hill clerked in a store, tried teaching, married, clerked in a store again, lived on a small farm. At

64

thirty-eight he couldn't stay away from the children any longer, and went back to teaching. Three years later, on the death of Stiles, his old principal, he succeeded to the post of county superintendent and stayed in that position until 1902.

He was sixty-eight when he turned the county schools over to Ralph Decker, but he had not yet achieved his greatest fame. Back on his Andover farm, with the time to take his garden seriously, he developed the strain of sweet corn which bears his name, and which many a Sussex Countyite will tell you is our greatest contribution so far to the culture and civilization of the world. Luther Hill, who gave his life to education, became immortal as a horticulturist!

4. The Automobile Changes Our Lives

Nineteen eleven was a big year for automobiles. Not the first year, of course. Cars had been seen around the County for eight or nine years. A summer resident at Blairstown had been seen driving her steamer — either a Stanley or a White — to Newton for weekend shopping since 1901 or thereabouts, and upsetting the placid life of the county seat no end. By 1911 everybody must have seen at least one car, and large numbers had ridden in them. Not everyone had had the opportunity to ride, and some had turned down the chance. Too risky!

Well, it **was** risky. Roads were either rutty, muddy, or dusty. They were narrow and often paralled by deep ditches. Upsetting was easy.

When it was dusty, such clouds would be raised as to make visibility poor and driving a hazard. On a breezeless, dusty Saturday afternoon in July, 1911, a large crowd went from Newton to Branchville by auto to see a baseball game. From hilltops along the route the course of the road could be traced for miles by the dust suspended over it.

Our first automobile accident occurred in 1911, and a dust screen was the cause. Fred Barnes was driving from Newton to Andover behind a Paterson car which was throwing dust and making it difficult to see anything. In the murk he struck Joseph Wintermute who, at twelve years of age, was riding his bike toward Newton. Joseph was scared, bruised, and banged, and his wheel was a total wreck. But that was all, luckily.

Steering mechanisms frequently broke down in 1911, and punctures and blowouts were expected, but these hazards were all a part of the sport, and that's what driving a motor vehicle was still in 1911. Of course, there were signs of commercialization. Lehman's, store proprietors in Dover and Newton, put into service in 1911 one of the first trucks seen in these parts. It was capable of carrying sixty crates of eggs and could go better than thirty-five miles per hour. It used to come whizzing up from Dover to Newton in an hour and twenty minutes.

When we talk about car costs in those days we must remember that $1,000 a year wasn't bad wages. By that measuring stick, prices were high. One of the most popular makes in Sussex County was the Buick, vigorously promoted by W. W. Woodward. Prices ranged from $585 for a topless, two-passenger runabout to $1,885 for the big four-door touring car. There were no closed models at all.

On Water St. in Newton J. F. Lovely and A. L. Pashby were agents for the Paige at the Sussex County Garage. This was a medium-priced car; tops for the four-door touring job was $995. In Lafayette J. Frank Backster opened up a Hupmobile agency. The Hup emphasized simplicity ("speeds smoothly away at the touch of one lever and two pedals") and sold for $900. But that was complete, which meant something. People who today complain about the added cost of "optional equipment" should have dickered for a car in 1911! Note the "extras": top, windshield, gas lamp, oil lamp generator, a set of tools, and doors. That's right — doors. Folks wouldn't have gone for safety belts back then; many of them did without doors, for when the car started to roll over, they wanted out.

There weren't many women drivers in 1911, but one who elicited much admiration for her dexterity and courage was Loretta Flock, daughter of a Hackettstown merchant, who used to drive each week to her job as organist at Newton Presbyterian Church. Her sister would come along to spell her on the homeward trick — driving from Hackettstown and back in one day was still considered too arduous for a woman.

"Runs" were big events in those primitive auto days, and the Sussex County Auto Club held its first in October, 1911. About twenty cars made the trip to Bertrand's Inn, Bernardsville, leaving Newton at one-minute intervals beginning at 9 a. m. They hit their target without mishap in about three hours, going by way of Stanhope, Dover, Parsippany, and Morristown. They came home by way of Lebanon, White House, Clinton, Washington, and Hackettstown.

Some of the club's members and hence the County's early auto enthusiasts were Thomas Bentley, Dr. Blase Cole, and Dr. E. Morrison, of Newton; Reeve Harden, Hamburg; Ford Margarum, Sussex; John Wills, Stanhope; M. D. Hayward, Branchville.

The Auto Club wasn't a social organization. It was a pressure group for road improvement, and between Morristown and Bernardsville they experienced a new type of road — macadam. They immediately began campaigning for some of that here, particularly on the Sparta-Stanhope road, in that day famous as the County's worst.

The new roads finally came. The new breed — auto drivers — saw to that. But before much could be done, the overseer system, by which a great number of men were each responsible individually for a certain section of the road, had to be abolished. Then some uniformity could be achieved.

One of the first to feel the effect of better roads were the schools. With school bus routes possible, consolidated schools were possible, and the one-room school was doomed.

At least one entire community, Lake Mohawk, first begun in 1926, would not have been attempted before the automobile age, and the improvement of the highway system since that time has seen Lake Mohawk and several other lake communities turn in a few years from strictly summer resorts into year-round communities within car commuting distance of metropolitan job opportunities.

The automobile also led directly to the establishment of the Selected Risks companies, the first of which entered the auto insurance field in 1926. Less dependent on the motor car, but still profiting from road construction have been firms like Limestone Products, which began operations in 1919.

Although our role as vacationland began as long ago as 1840 or earlier, it has been the automobile era that has given impetus to the development of High Point Park, Stokes State Forest, and other state parks and recreation areas within our borders. High Point, 11,061 acres, was a gift to the state in 1928 from Col. and Mrs. A. R. Kuser. The 220-foot monument is on New Jersey's highest point, 1,803 feet above sea level.

Stokes State Forest, named for a onetime N. J. governor, is 12,495 acres. Other state parks wholly or partly within the County are Cranberry Lake, Musconetcong Lake, Hopatcong, Swartswood. The state also owns 6,373 acres of public shooting and fishing grounds within the County.

Besides these direct results of the gasoline age, the indirect, often unrealized modifications which motor vehicles have made in our whole culture are incalculable. Sussex County's geographical situation has enabled us to get the most from the automobile.

5. Where Do We Go From Here?

Ever since I first became interested in Sussex County history I have been impressed with the way our people have adapted themselves to economic change. From an iron-based economy they turned, when forced by circumstances, to zinc mining in the Franklin-Sterling area and to agriculture in the rest of the County. When hogs and butter no longer brought an income, they learned to produce milk more efficiently.

What's next? The end of the dairy industry has been proclaimed for years, and it hasn't come yet, but it can probably not be staved off much longer. Zinc mining is done at Franklin and continues somewhat precariously at Sterling. Only good zinc prices make the operation possible. And, at any rate, mining no longer has a major impact on our economy.

Where do we go from here?

There are three coming events that seem to me must figure heavily in determining the shape of our future.

First, the Tocks Island development. This dam in the Delaware, with its resulting large lake and surrounding recreational area, will form the most popular of all national parks, with visitors figured as high as nine million a year. The benefits accruing to Sussex County can be tremendous; the problems generated will be enormous.

Second, the development of the state and interstate highway system, including the completion of Route 80, the dualization of Routes 23 and 206, and other highway improvements already planned for. Not only will these additions make us desirable as a residential area for countless commuters, but plant site locations will be seeking us out in increasing numbers.

Third. We live now on the northern edge of a vast metropolitan complex, a teeming city that ignores political lines and stretches as a single long, narrow community from Boston to Washington. It is a rapidly growing community that seems destined to widen until we are included. It is possible that we will be swept along by a tide of urbanization so strong, so compelling, that our best-laid plans to remain rural and residential will come to naught.

But that is the view of the pessimist, and it is not the view which is suggested by our history. Everything in our past shows us that every corner we have turned, however unwillingly, has opened up new opportunities to us. Always Sussex County has found a way.

Once again we are turning a corner. Who can doubt a bright new road awaits us?

About the Author

My home town is Lambertville, N. J., where I lived all my young life, although I was born in Riverton, N. J., in 1910, and where my mother is living now. Incidentally, Riverton is where the Japanese beetle also first saw the light of day in this country, but that was in 1915, and I got here first.

After college at Trenton State College, I came to Newton to teach high school English in the fall of 1930, and here I still am. In my first ten years in the county I acquired a master's degree (Rutgers) and a wife, who is a member of one of the old Sussex County families. In my second ten years I acquired a son and an additional job with the State Department of Education. All of these I still have.

In the third ten years I acquired a job with the old Sussex Independent writing a weekly column of local history. At first it was a chore that paid money, but soon I was hooked, found it fascinating, and kept it up for 80-odd weeks, until the Herald bought the Independent.

Right now the two extra jobs that occupy me most are serving as president of the Sussex County Education Association and as admissions chairman of the Farm and Horse Show.

I now have a wife, a son, a cat, a car, a house in Newton, a cottage in Hardyston Township, a job. I am a Methodist, a liberal Republican, a Mets fan, and take both sugar and cream. In my coffee, that is.

Warren D. Cummings

About the Illustrators

The Rutherfords, who have done the illustrations for this book, were both born in Minnesota.

Bonnie was raised in Idaho, Bill grew up in Minnesota. They met while studying at the Minneapolis School of Art, and after graduation were married.

Both received Ethel Morrison VanDerlip scholarships for further study and travel. They choose to study at the Art Student's League in New York.

Later they began their career as an illustrating team and chose Sussex County for their permanent home where they live in Frankford Township with their four children.

A Word About Sources

"Where do you find all that stuff?" people always want to know. Sources of information run all the way from conversations to tombstones, but here are a few of the many, many books that I've read that have been most helpful to me:

Snell's *History of Sussex and Warren Counties* is basic information for anybody wanting to know this county at all well.

Edsall's *Centennial Address* is absolutely indispensable. As I have said in the text, Ben Edsall did the original digging for facts. And all of us, from Snell to me, have borrowed from him.

Swayze's *Historical Address,* made in 1903, extends Edsall for fifty years. It was Swayze who found a lot of "firsts"—the first baseball game, the first gas lights, and many more.

Gordon's *Gazetteer and History of New Jersey,* published in 1834, is the book that got me started. When I was about fourteen, I bought at a sale a solid cherry five-shelf bookcase full of books for $2.50! Gordon was one of the books, and it has been one of my prize possessions ever since. It was Gordon who first won my interest in New Jersey history.

Shuster's *Historical Notes of the Iron and Zinc Mining Industry in Sussex County, New Jersey* tells the story of the mines at Franklin and Ogdensburg in great detail. Mayor Shuster makes most of it understandable even to a layman like me.

Decker's *Then and Now* gives the story of our schools from 1902 until 1942. It has a wealth of old photographs.

Agriculture in Sussex County in 1945 by the Vocational School of Agriculture has some invaluable material in the field of farming.

Undoubtedly the greatest bulk of my information has come from the old files of *The New Jersey Herald,* the *Sussex Register,* and the *Sussex Independent.* To the editors of these weeklies I owe a real debt of gratitude.

Warren D. Cummings